T0361490

ALSO BY JACQUELINE ROSE

THE PLAGUE

THE PLAGUE

LIVING DEATH IN OUR TIMES

Jacqueline Rose

FARRAR, STRAUS AND GIROUX

NEW YORK

Farrar, Straus and Giroux
120 Broadway, New York 10271

Printed in the United States of America
Originally published in 2023 by Fitzcarraldo Editions, Great Britain
Published in the United States by Farrar, Straus and Giroux
First American edition, 2023

Library of Congress Cataloging-in-Publication Data
Names: Rose, Jacqueline, author.
Title: The plague : living death in our times / Jacqueline Rose.
Description: First American edition. | New York : Farrar, Straus and
    Giroux, 2023. |
Identifiers: LCCN 2023008661 | ISBN 9780374610869 (hardcover)
Subjects: LCSH: Plague—Psychological aspects. | Plague—Social aspects. |
    Death. | Death—Psychological aspects. | COVID-19 Pandemic, 2020—
    Psychological aspects.
Classification: LCC RC171 .R57 2023 | DDC 614.5/732—dc23/eng/
    20230406
LC record available at https://lccn.loc.gov/2023008661

Designed by Patrice Sheridan

Our books may be purchased in bulk for promotional, educational, or business
use. Please contact your local bookseller or the Macmillan Corporate and
Premium Sales Department at 1-800-221-7945, extension 5442, or by email at
MacmillanSpecialMarkets@macmillan.com.

www.fsgbooks.com
www.twitter.com/fsgbooks • www.facebook.com/fsgbooks

1   3   5   7   9   10   8   6   4   2

For J,
Whatever the weather—

We are not really without hope. The mere fact that we exist, that we conceive and want something different from what exists, constitutes a reason for hope.

—Simone Weil, *Oppression and Liberty* (1933)

May I be alive when I die.

—D. W. Winnicott, *Unfinished Autobiography* (1971)

CONTENTS

THE PLAGUE

INTRODUCTION:

THE WAY IN

THIS BOOK HAS BEEN written in the heat and chill of its moment. It begins with the first UK pandemic lockdown in March 2020 and then takes us forward to barely two years later, when Vladimir Putin's invasion of Ukraine had just begun. As I write these pages, war has broken out in the heart of Europe, shattering the illusion, partly fostered by the pandemic, that the world is united in the struggle against needless dying. Such unity was in any case a myth, honed to Western privilege and blindness, as the slew of wars across less newsworthy continents—from Yemen to Syria to Ethiopia—so clearly testifies. One of the most difficult aspects of these past years has been to square what felt at the start like a new global solidarity in response to the pandemic with the inequalities which slowly, or not so slowly, rose to the surface of public life, exposing the brute vulnerability of the subordinate, marginal, oppressed and the poor. No amount of common purpose has been able to thwart the power of wealth and status to determine who lives and who dies—whether in the guise of big pharma blocking patent waivers on Covid-19 vaccinations, or the surge in domestic violence, or the daily threat of racist killings on the streets. The pandemic struck like a force of nature, but, like the climate catastrophe, it also laid bare just how far nature is a plaything of human whim.

And then, as Russia's violence in Ukraine ratcheted up on a daily basis, the world found itself faced with the megalomaniac tyranny of state boldly proclaiming its capacity to destroy the world. When violence takes the form of tanks on the street, we can no longer assign it to the heavens. One of the strangest and most perverse gifts of war is its capacity to shred any delusion that death is somehow random and innocent of human calculation. Instead, death belongs at the heart of the very legal authority to which we have been appealing to subdue it. In reality, death is always stalking among us, at once the starkest measure of unjust social arrangements, the prized monopoly of statecraft, and a reminder of the limits of human power.

What do you do with death and dying when they can no longer be pushed to the outer limits of your lived experience or dismissed from your conscious mind? How do you live with death or rather how do you 'live death'—a formula which might seem at first glance to defy understanding—when death comes too close, pervading the air you breathe? In what follows, 'living death' will appear as something of a refrain, a reminder that to think of death as an avoidable intruder into how we order our lives, especially in the West, is an act of defiance that is doomed to fail. In the thought of the philosopher Simone Weil, it is only in admitting the limits of the human that we will stop vaunting the brute illusion of earthly power, as if we owned the world we live in.

Perhaps, then, if those limits were acknowledged, the world would look less murderous. Killing is one of the most effective, but also desperate and self-defeating, ways of warding off one's own death (a fantasy demonstrated by the need of serial killers to kill over and over again). For Putin, being president for life is not enough. He is aiming for the stars. The goal to finish off Russia is 'centuries old and unchanging', according to pro-Kremlin news host Dmitry Kiselyov. In the words of Ukrainian writer Oleksandr Mykhed, Russia is a country that 'lives by the holy conviction that it will exist for ever'. It is in the name of 'eternal Russia' that missiles rain down on Ukraine (even if the Western powers had up to this war preferred to treat Putin as a rational technocrat with whom they could do business). Dictators always believe—or rather act as if they believe—that they are invincible, although somewhere they know this to be a lie. Which is why they respond to every sign of possible failure—a forty-mile convoy of Russian tanks, which Ukraine could never match, grinding to a halt in the early spring mud at the outset of the war—by lashing out even more. Like warriors, what invading armies want, Weil writes in perhaps her most famous essay, 'The *Iliad*, or the Poem of Force', is 'everything'. 'They forget one detail, that *everything* is not within their power.' For the Russian people, any victory will be hollow. They will be left with the death bowl of their dreams.

We need a different mental dispensation, one that does not flatten the world to its own worst contours but rather bends and moves against the grain, following the most sinuous, risky and creative pathways of the mind. Can we imagine a world in which the deepest respect for death would exist alongside a fairer distribution of the wealth of the earth so that each individual has their share? How can we ensure that death, as much as life, is given its dignity? How to honour the nameless Covid-stricken corpses burning in the night on the streets of Indian cities, or the woman in Kyiv spooning the shards of glass from her shattered balcony window while her building, its foundations blasted to pieces, teeters on the verge of collapse? These images are just two of the many that have haunted me over these past years, raising questions to which I return repeatedly in what follows. What can we ask of the polity in apocalyptic, plague-ridden times, when the worst of such times has manifestly arisen out of the decisions of the polity itself? What can we ask, or rather what should we be asking, of ourselves?

As a school pupil studying Albert Camus's *The Plague*, I never imagined that one day—more than half a century later—I would find myself returning to the novel along with hundreds of thousands of other readers the world over. I was seeking guidance through the pandemic, a reality which up till then I had firmly assigned to a bygone age (in fact, the novel was published two years before I was born). Nor did this belief stem simply from the prehistoric ring which attaches to the very idea of a 'plague': black death, bubonic plague, the plagues of Egypt. In fact, Camus takes the Second World War as his analogy for the plague, overlaying two drastic histories, one of which, the war, shadowed my early life at the same time as being rarely, if ever, spoken about. Reading his novel gave me perhaps my first glimmer of understanding that something can be shrouded in silence and press even harder on everyday life as a result. It taught me how cleverly defensive and self-blinding are the capacities of the human mind. Perhaps the most difficult thing to acknowledge is the fact that, however inexplicable the arrival of a plague or pandemic might feel, however indiscriminately death-dealing, it is part of history, something which human societies and those who make up their number bring upon themselves.

This book therefore opens with Camus's novel. If it felt—still feels—so disturbingly relevant to Covid-19 and its aftermath, this is because it recounts a form of disaster which requires almost super-human vigilance if it is ever to go away (for that reason Camus thinks it never will). 'We are all carriers' ('*pestiférés*'), states Tarrou, one of the central characters in the book. We are all complicit in so far as each one of us turns a blind eye to death and dying every day, including death in our own name, that is death in the hands of the state (Tarrou's father was a judge who sent criminals to execution). In the modern Western world, people are prone to treating death as everyone's problem but their own—hence the joke, cited by Freud, where the husband blithely says to his wife: 'When one of us dies, I will move to Paris' (the ultimate throw-away line). What is the relationship between such careless denial of death, not to speak of its barely concealed hostility, and the flagrant precision with which death spreads across the earth? Writing in 1940, at the outset of the war, the British psychoanalyst D. W. Winnicott suggested that the hardest path for the individual to follow 'is for him to see that all the greed, aggression and deceit in the world *might have been* his own responsibility, even if in point of fact it is not' (his emphasis). Everyone is accountable or should behave as if they were. Pandemics threaten to bring—or should bring—to the forefront of human consciousness, the extent to which we are all responsible for each other. Pandemics can strike at any time but, as Camus suggests with startling foresight, they only do so when the putrefaction of a neglectful, arbitrary and inhuman world breaks through the defences which serve to hold that world unjustly in its place. The two realities of history which to date people have never been prepared for—both of which have come crashing into our daylight hours over these past years—are, he states without hesitation, plagues and wars. What more might have been done to prevent them? It will always remain something of a mystery how, as they go about their daily business, people manage to smother and sweep the harshest realities out of their heads.

Every year the Vienna Freud Memorial Lecture is held annually on Freud's birthday, 6 May. When the 2020 lecture, which I had been invited to deliver, had to be postponed due to Covid-19, it made perfect, although somewhat disquieting, sense that Monika Pessler, the Sigmund Freud Museum's Director, suggested it should be moved to 23 September, the day he died. Given the situation in which we found ourselves, it seemed right that the theme of death, which had tracked Freud's thinking while undergoing monumental upheavals in the course of his work, should be the subject I would talk about. Because of Covid travel restrictions, I delivered the lecture livestreamed from the Freud Museum in London in a room with no audience.

I was to stand between two couches, one immediately recognizable as the couch which, since the opening of the museum, had always graced Freud's consulting room. The couch on the other side I had never seen before. Minutes before we began, Carol Siegel, the London director, told me that it was the couch on which he had died. It seemed appropriate, not just to the historic crisis we were all living, but also to my topic that, in the space of a split second, any of the internal equipoise which I thought I had summoned to deliver the lecture pretty much fell to pieces.

Anyone writing about Covid, and again during the Russian invasion of Ukraine, will, I suspect, have had their version of this experience, where the acute reality of the hour makes any control over words, indeed any semblance of self-mastery, seem even more fraudulent than usual. This is just one reason why the injunction to carry on as normal—or return to normal—as fast as possible, which was the supreme driver of then-UK Prime Minister Boris Johnson's political and personal agenda, seemed not just to fly in the face of all evidence but was also felt to be such an insult. Grappling with death had become our daily fare and obligation, although it is one that so many world leaders from Johnson to Jair Bolsonaro to Narendra Modi appeared to hate (almost as if it were a personal affront). Johnson was therefore by no means alone in this although he was, I would say, one of the worst. Like Trump, he is dishonest to the core. Even more important than his personal failings, however, was the fact that the entire political atmosphere he promoted—feel good, pretend the worst isn't happening—was a barefaced lie. We have been living a war of (psychic) attrition: told on a more or less daily basis that the situation can be managed, while, to take just the most glaring example, the NHS crumbled (as relentlessly charted by palliative care doctor Rachel Clarke among others, though it was obvious to anyone who had eyes to see). After every temporary reprieve, the toll of infection mounted once more—most recently the surge of summer 2022, which the government in the UK chose more or less completely to ignore, while as I write, a new Omicron variant, starting in India, is being reported across the globe (cases reported in the UK, US, Germany, and Canada). Consigning Covid to history, surveillance and testing capabilities have been dropped by countries across the world.

Under such pretence and obfuscation, what happens to the idea that being human is to be irrevocably in touch with both intimate and social pain? At moments it has felt to me that we are being asked to participate in a collective psychosis—where the gap between inner life and the reality of the world around us is being pulled further and further apart, at the same time as the walls around what it is permissible to think, say, and do have started to close in. To take just two examples of the second: a new law cracking down on public protest in the UK; inhuman asylum policies now stalling entry to Ukrainian refugees (not to speak of the plan to send refugees on a one-way ticket to offshore camps in Rwanda). In Freud's famous distinction, the neurotic represses, or tries to repress, that part of their desire which clashes with reality; the psychotic withdraws from reality and moulds their sense of the outside world to harmonize with their delusions. Hence the famous resistance of psychotic disturbance to negotiation and cure. Although the Austro-British psychoanalyst Melanie Klein would prove him wrong, Freud felt that psychosis was beyond the reach of psychoanalytic treatment. I have lost count of the number of times over these past years when it has felt as if those in power, without a tremor of self-doubt, were inviting us to enter the bubble of a world gone completely mad.

In 1926, Klein arrived in London, introduced into the British psychoanalytic community by Freud's future biographer, Ernest Jones. Just over a decade later in 1938, Freud, in flight from the Nazis, escaped Austria to London accompanied by his daughter, the psychoanalyst Anna Freud. Psychoanalysis therefore made its way into the UK under the shadow of past and impending war. Plague had also been its bedfellow, although this is less known. In 1920, Freud's favourite daughter, Sophie Halberstadt-Freud, died during the fourth wave of the so-called 'Spanish' flu, which had ravaged Europe for several years and which also played its part in determining the outcome of the First World War. Before it struck, the Axis powers were confident of victory. Freud therefore found himself in the midst of the two experiences, plague and war, for which Camus believed no one is ever prepared. As we will see, Freud was no exception. These are two writers linked across the divide between knowledge that can and cannot be borne. By far the worst pandemic of the twentieth century, with a death toll higher than the two world wars combined, the Spanish flu has been more or less erased from history. Excavating this history, tracing the impact of his daughter's death on Freud's understanding of the human mind, is to register the uncanny and persistent ease of historical forgetting against which the whole of psychoanalysis pitches itself.

———

The third figure whom I offer here as a guide through these times is the extraordinary French thinker and writer Simone Weil. Perhaps coincidentally, more likely not, she completes the circuit of the book by leading us back to Camus. He was one of the first to recognize her writing, admiring her at a time when her truly prodigious output was barely known. In 1943 at the age of thirty-four, Weil died in a hospital in London where she had been waiting to cross the Channel and join the French Resistance. She had fallen ill with tuberculosis, which became incurable when she refused to eat any more than the pitiful rations of food available to her co-patriots fighting in France. She was also grief-stricken that her plan to parachute a troop of nurses into occupied France to tend the sick and the dying, a plan she managed to have brought to the attention of Charles de Gaulle, had been dismissed by him as insane.

Weil knew exactly what she was asking for. She acknowledged that the nurses would most likely die alongside their patients and would know this. But she also had confidence in what she described as a unique brand of determination, possessed by some women who risk their lives in the service of care. Such an act would offer the world at war an irrefutable moral example from which the enemy would be unable to recover. This 'cold, virile' determination is rarely found, she suggested, 'in the same human being together with the tenderness required to comfort suffering and the agony of death. But no matter how rare, it can be found.' She could be describing nurses and care workers during the pandemic, or those making their way to tend the mortally wounded in cities under bombardment in Ukraine. It was, she elaborated, a form of courage which, unlike the fatal bravado of wartime, was not 'kindled' by the desire to kill, but by the ability and willingness to bear the sight of the dying. For Weil, this vision was merely an extension of every human's obligation to the most vulnerable people in the world which means accepting their frailty and mortality as one's own. It was also where she grounded her ethics of love. Bearing the thought that a loved one is mortal, she wrote in her 1941–1942 notebook in Marseille, the first stop in her flight from Nazi-occupied Paris, 'might indeed have died at the very moment one is thinking about them', is in itself an act of love (she was in the midst of the war, but she could equally have been writing about a pandemic).

Weil's prescience here seems remarkable. For more than two years, fear of contagion has dominated airwaves across the globe, only to be suddenly and carelessly usurped by war. The two are linked, not just as Camus suggested by how unprepared people have historically been for both, but also for the way they pit humans against each other. Shun the contagious, kill the enemy—such brutal instructions are always in danger of becoming the norm (fear of contagion as the antithesis of care). As if, they each imply, the first step towards a liveable life, or even the only way to survive, is to draw up a list of those to be killed and/or ostracized. For Weil, on the other hand, the only viable path to justice was to make common cause with those who 'do not count', not 'in any situation, in anyone's eyes'—the exploited and destitute, the criminal reoffender, the racial minority, the outcast, the sick, the refugee—those whose fate the more fortunate are desperate to avoid, those they least want to be. Crucially, in the world of Homer, which was so important to Weil, Zeus, on whose law justice depends, extends his protection above all to those whose place in the established order of things is uncertain—the stranger and the suppliant.

Weil was calling for a radical new form of equality. One that trusts in the ability of hearts and minds to cut across national, class and racial bounds. Her description of class exploitation has lost none of its force; she herself worked in factories in order to experience the affliction of the workers at first hand. What she found was a form of living death, what she sought was a world in which nobody would ever find themselves in conditions which made it preferable to die. Her condemnation of French colonialism for trampling over indigenous peoples was without reserve. If France failed to relinquish its colonies, she insisted, any victory against Nazism would fail. She came close to predicting ecological disaster. Society was weighing on humanity 'more cruelly than water, earth, air and fire', all the more so as it wrests the elements to its purpose, while capital expansion was heading for the point where it would be 'halted by the actual limits of the earth's surface' (or not halted as billionaires today launch themselves into space). Her belief in democracy was as steadfast as it was wary. Democracies whose main aim is to overthrow democracy itself (Hitler's Germany) 'stifle their own breath' when they introduce discriminatory laws, but if they fail to do so, they will be 'as safe as a little bird in front of a snake'. Nations that deny their own violent histories, notably imperial crimes, are as foolishly destructive 'as a child tearing the petals off a rose' (she was agitator and poet).

One by one, as we will see, Weil puts in place the building blocks of the most heated political struggles and debates that stretch across the world today: the fight for decolonization and for the legacy of slavery to be remembered; the calling out of corruption and coercion in democracies that boast their freedom; or, in the opposite direction, the preposterous suggestion, made by the former UK Home Secretary, Priti Patel, shortly after the Russian invasion, that Ukrainian refugees fleeing a war zone should be barred entry for fear of Russian infiltrators (another threat of contagion to add to all the rest). What might a nation look like, Weil asks, that is grounded in love for the alien, something which to this day has never been seen? What unthinkable shifts in the mental weather are needed for the world in which we are living to survive? A form of sainthood, she concedes. But then in the midst of a catastrophic world war which she hated, perhaps sainthood was in order 'just as doctors are needed in a city stricken with plague'. None of this got in the way of her analysis of the irresistible temptation of power at its most lethal, which pushes anyone who wields it to exceed all human restraint. If the Russian military are committing atrocities in Ukraine, one reporter on the ground observed, it is simply because, like its American and British counterparts, 'they can'. Weil's work can be read as a manifesto. She is laying out just how much is needed to remedy social destruction and to avoid the worst of who we are. 'Each of us,' she writes, is tempted to set his failings to one side, 'to stuff them into the attic,' but 'to give way to this temptation is to ruin the soul.' She is talking of individual human subjects and of nations.

———

As I am writing, universities in England are experiencing the worst assault on the humanities that I can remember in my lifetime (and there have been a few). No one I know doubts for one minute that this is a reaction to the role that universities are playing in creating a space for social critique at a time when it has never been more needed. To take just one example, universities are at the forefront of the cry for decolonization on campus, for memory and redress in relation to slavery and subjugation, which Weil was advocating those many years ago. As a student in Oxford at the time of the student uprisings of 1968, I for one have never lost my conviction that universities should be at the vanguard of such struggles, and that providing an education in dissent, critique and activism is a role that any self-respecting institution of learning should play. Today these aims are written into the objectives of a new global university, the Open Society University Network, launched by George Soros in 2020 after his Central European University was hounded out of Hungary by anti-Semitism (an educational initiative to which Birkbeck together with the Birkbeck Institute for the Humanities are proud to be associated). I remember responding with genuine bafflement when a senior academic told me, in response to '68, that students were not at university to engage in politics, as if that were not a core part of their education into citizenship. The same objecting voices can be heard even more loudly today (for me, telling a student not to be political is like instructing a swimmer to stay on dry land).

At the core of this battle is the question of what thought is capable of. How far, in whatever circumstances, are we willing, or able, to let ourselves go into the unacceptable and unspoken reaches of the world and of the mind? This, of course, is where Freud's work and psychoanalysis begins, the mental place into which pandemics and wars could be said to push just about everyone. Freedom of thought is most often taken to mean the freedom to say whatever we please without fear of censure. But there is another meaning, no less important, which is the ability to track by means of thought the more hidden, painful and scandalous aspects of human life in a world which has turned—or so it has seemed repeatedly over these past years—even more dangerous and cruel than it was before (again this might have special poignancy for the generation of '68 who believed the world could be moulded to their dreams).

For Weil, there is something intrinsically radical in the power of thought. Because a human is a thinking creature, 'never, whatever may happen', will mankind accept servitude. Thought can be revolutionary or counter-revolutionary, but in so far as it goes beyond the world as known and seen, it is always the enemy of domination. Like love, thinking is 'corrosive' for the social order. 'The powerful forces that we have to fight are preparing to crush us,' she acknowledged, 'but they cannot stop us from working towards a clear comprehension of the object of our efforts.' It was a refrain. However bad things get, 'nothing in the world can prevent us from thinking clearly,' 'nothing can compel anyone to exercise their powers of thought or take away their powers over their own mind.' I think it is fair to say that she was talking about herself. In the times we are living, when it can feel almost impossible to avoid despair, I have tried—as indeed throughout all that follows—to take her brief and run with it.

THE PLAGUE

AS SOON AS COVID-19 fully hit public consciousness—in Western Europe roughly from the end of January 2020—sales of Albert Camus's *The Plague*, a novel first published in 1947, grew exponentially, an upsurge strangely in tandem with the graphs proffered on a daily basis to chart the toll of the sick and the dead. According to the publisher of the UK Penguin Classics edition, by the end of March 2020, monthly sales had increased from the low hundreds to the mid-thousands and continued to rise. In relation to the spread of the virus, such tallies are always approximate and imperfect, but this reality appears to remove none of their quasi-sacred status. As if intoning numbers according to the same recognizable formula, however scary, allowed us to feel on top of a situation which everyone knew—and not just because of government incompetence—was out of our control. One of the things *The Plague* conveys is how, in the very moment we appear to be facing the grimmest reality, we might also be deluding ourselves. Counting is at once a scientific endeavour and a form of magical thinking. It can be a means of confronting and bracing the onslaught and, at the same time, a doomed gesture of omnipotence, a system for classifying and bundling the horror away. What exactly are we being told every day when the figures are announced, rising consistently, dropping slightly, increasing again—other than that we cannot get a grip on what is happening? We take the measures that are there to be taken, adequate and inadequate according to where and who we are. And we wait.

In the novel, it is only when men, as opposed to hundreds of rats, start dying that the public begins to understand. And even then, only slowly. The announcement of three hundred and two dead citizens in the third week does not speak to the public imagination: 'The plague was unimaginable, or rather it was being imagined in the wrong way.' As Camus put it in his composition notebooks of 1938, the people are 'lacking in imagination . . . They don't think on the right scale for plagues. And the remedies they think up are barely suitable for a head cold. They will die (develop).' Perhaps, it is suggested, not all these deaths were attributable to the plague. What would be the number of weekly deaths for a population the size of such a city in the normal run of things? These are almost the exact formulae that were reached for by Donald Trump and Jair Bolsonaro in their earliest denial mode (from which the Brazilian President never budged). In Camus's rendering, however, such thinking should not simply be dismissed as the ranting of dangerous fools, which it also clearly was, and is. Camus is interested in how human subjects deal with disaster. Denial, or defence, is an integral part of how the mind works. Wars and plagues are both met with disbelief, first, that they are happening at all, and, secondly, given their affront to human dignity—their 'stupidity' to use Camus's word—that they will endure: 'There have been as many plagues as wars in history, yet always wars and plagues take people equally by surprise.' 'It was only as time passed, and the rise in the steady death rate could not be ignored, that public opinion came alive to the truth.'

And yet, for Camus, it is also a form of creativity to craft the world beyond the agonies of the hour, to refuse to submit to the indiscriminate calculations of number, which mimic the merciless logic of the plague itself. The first real sign that the disease might be nearing its end comes when the numbers start to flounder and no longer add up or make any sense: a rising number of deaths on Mondays, while on Wednesdays, for some inexplicable reason, hardly any at all; hundreds still dying in one district, others from which the plague seems to have quietly slipped away. The plague, the narrator comments, was losing 'its self-command, the ruthless almost mathematical efficiency that had been its trump card hitherto.' Mathematics flattens. It is a killing art. Counting humans, alive or dead, means you have entered a world of abstraction—things have taken a desperate turn. Of course counting can also mean the exact opposite. If someone counts, it means they matter, with the further implication that they can be held answerable for their own deeds. Not to count, on the other hand, is to be overlooked or invisible, like the Arabs of Oran, whose absence from Camus's portrayal of the French Algerian town where the novel takes place is generally recognized as the most significant failing of his tale; more than a hundred thousand were living in Oran at the time.

'Counting' might, then, fall under the rubric of what Freud described as the 'antithetical meaning of primal words' characteristic of the most ancient Egyptian languages, words which simultaneously denote one thing and its opposite, and which also have a type of magic, since they release you into a world of contradiction and mystery that is incalculable and only partly known. To utter such words always carries a risk. The meaning you least intend hovers barely beneath the level of consciousness, ready to pounce like the plague which, Camus insists, even after it has abated, has never gone away. Instead, it patiently bides its time in 'bedrooms, cellars, trunks, handkerchiefs and old papers, until the day comes when, for the misery and edification of mankind, it awakens its rats and sends them forth to die in a happy city' (the last lines of the novel). In *The Plague*, the pestilence is at once blight and revelation. It brings the hidden truth of a corrupt world order into view. This is hinted at very early on, when the soft corpses of dead rats are being felt underfoot in the night, but before any humans have died:

> It was as if the earth on which our houses were planted was being purged of its secreted humours, thrusting up to the surfaces the abscesses and pus-clots that, up till then, had been doing their work internally. Imagine the amazement of our little city, hitherto so tranquil and now shaken to its core in a matter of days, like a healthy man who all of a sudden feels a revolutionary surge in his thick blood.

The novel's first English translator, Stuart Gilbert, translated 'doing their work internally'—the French is *'travaillaient intérieurement'*—as 'that had been forming in its entrails'. This is more visceral but it loses the ambiguity of the French *'intérieurement'* which leaves open whether what is being referred to are the restless innards of the body or the ructions of the unconscious mind.

In a 2020 interview, French analyst and theorist Julia Kristeva described how the telephone sessions made obligatory by the pandemic, which hold the voice at a new distance, are helping reticent patients speak of deep forms of memory and distress—the early death of a mother from cancer, abuse or abandonment as a child—which they had never been able to access or articulate before. Cities also have their secrets which, like the plague, can seem to erupt out of nowhere. In the last piece she wrote before she was gunned down on the streets in the Creggan area of Derry, Northern Ireland, journalist Lyra McKee described how the peace process had enforced a collective amnesia in relation to earlier violence which was now haunting the present 'like a ghost that refused to depart for the other world'. The greatest betrayal was the promise made by politicians that 'the days of young people disappearing and dying young would be gone'. The article was published in *The Guardian* on 28 March 2020, one week into lockdown, which added to its strange aura of foreboding, as if McKee had been warning us that we were about to enter, or re-enter, a state of war.

In his translation, Gilbert also drops the reference to 'revolution' (*'comme un homme bien-portant dont le sang épais se mettrait tout d'un coup en révolution*'), which he renders more poetically as 'the blood seething like wildfire in his veins.' This is a real loss. 'Revolution' points towards Camus's *L'homme révolté*, the 1951 book that followed *The Plague* and whose English title—*The Rebel*—again sidesteps the key element of revolution, as well as that of disgust. All revolt involves 'revulsion', writes Camus in the opening chapter, 'the categorical refusal of an intrusion felt to be intolerable'. In *The Plague* the two feelings are inseparable, as is captured most succinctly in an exchange between the physician Bernard Rieux, the central character who reveals himself to be the novel's narrator at the end, and Father Paneloux, who preaches acquiescence and divine love to packed congregations of the fearful, while also himself joining the fight against the plague to which he finally succumbs. They have just watched the drawn-out death throes of a young child whom they believed they could save:

> "There are times when the only feeling I have is one of mad revolt."
>
> "I understand," Paneloux said in a low voice. "That kind of thing is revolting because it passes our human understanding. But perhaps we should love what we cannot understand."
>
> "No, Father. I've a very different idea of love. And until my dying day I shall refuse to love a scheme of things in which children are put to torture."

The plague sparks a revolution in the blood. It erupts like a protest or insurrection, offering a fleeting moment of lucidity in an unjust world. Seen in this light, the novel could be read as issuing a warning or asking a question, one which drives many responses to the world laid bare by Covid-19: under what—extreme—conditions can the truth of social deprivation be recognized? 'The lockdown worked like a chemical experiment,' writes Arundhati Roy, 'that suddenly revealed hidden things,' as India's working-class citizens and migrant workers were spewed out of the rich towns and mega-cities 'like so much unwanted accrual'. In the UK, many of us were taken aback by the sudden, complete unravelling of austerity, which started more or less the morning after Boris Johnson's election victory of December 2019—although everyone knows that the move was part of his bid for re-election, a way of keeping on board the Midlands voters who had merely lent him their votes. No one could have predicted that the policy would be so magnified by the crisis, as ministers tripped over themselves in their eagerness to declare an end to Thatcherite shibboleths, by nationalizing and bailing out industries, flooding the NHS with millions of pounds and inscribing worker protections into law, although most of these initiatives have been rowed back in the years that have followed.

Just for a moment, it felt as if the wool had been lifted from their eyes and a whole order of exploitation and inequality might just—or so we hoped—come to an end. Even though this brings us perilously close to the idea that a miracle can arise from a curse and that all the suffering will have been worth it (Camus is unequivocal that nothing can justify the suffering caused by the plague). But something was being registered to which many had turned a blind eye before. Shortly after the fall of the Berlin Wall, a friend in New York described to me how the poor had suddenly become visible on the city streets, whereas, before 1989, just to mention them was to be tarred immediately with the brush of communism. Camus was tormented by the question of what humankind is capable of doing, or permitting, with open eyes. He wrote *L'homme révolté* in the 1940s because he 'could not understand how men could torture others while continuing to look at them'.

One of the ironies of the time has been the idea, cried from the rooftops, that 'we' are all in this together, at the very same moment that social disparity—the frailty of that 'we'—has never been so clear as the gulf widened: between families with gardens and those in airless, cladded, tower blocks, a distinction disregarded by police rounding on people in the parks; between the jogging culture of North London and the slums of Bangladesh where the idea of social distancing, let alone of soap and hand sanitizers in abundance, is some kind of sick joke; between the medical care lavished on the Prime Minister when he went down with Covid in May 2020, assigned an ICU bed at a time of acute shortage while still fit enough—or so we were first told—to govern, and the negligence suffered by nurse Thomas Harvey of East London who, after twenty years of service in the NHS, was denied an ambulance (the family called four times) and died gasping for air in his bathroom.

Oddly, the panic-buying of this era served to detract attention from the more basic problem of maintaining the food supply in times of pestilence and war—another thing the two crises have in common. The UK mandates to 'buy less' or 'only buy your fair share' focused on individual greed—if only people restrained themselves, everyone would still be living in a world of plenty. Stories of robberies and attacks on supermarkets in the poorest area of Southern Italy—where people faced a real risk of starvation—barely made it into the news in the UK, suggesting that the only deaths worth reporting were the result of the pandemic. As if nobody were dying before. This is not so unusual. Writing in the middle of the First World War, Freud had noted the modern tendency to treat all deaths as woeful exceptions, rather than as something that we all get round to in time. When the issue of supply is raised, it tends to be part of a discussion—which is of course needed—about the possibly irreparable damage that has been wrought by globalization to the food chain. The breaks in that chain may well be one cause of the virus travelling with such alacrity from plant life or from other living species to humans. 'Our getting and spending,' Rebecca Solnit observed, 'has been a kind of war against the Earth.' The point is that in all of this, no one yet knows whether the world after Covid-19 will be more attuned to climate change, and will take the measures required, however drastic, or if the exploitation of natural resources will merely accelerate to make up for lost time.

In Camus's novel, people starve. As the profiteers move in to take advantage of shortages, the yawning gulf between rich and poor gapes wider than before: 'Profiteers were taking a hand and purveying at enormous prices essential foodstuffs not available in the shops. The result was that poor families were in great straits, while the rich went short of practically nothing.' It is a delusion to suggest that death is the great equalizer: 'Thus whereas plague through its impartial ministrations should have promoted equality among our city's folk, it now had the opposite effect and, thanks to the normal play of different forms of selfishness, it sharpened the sense of injustice in the hearts of mankind.' When the poor of Oran take to the streets brandishing the slogan 'Bread or air', their demonstrations are met with instant and brutal suppression. Camus is crying injustice. The plague is, or should be, an opportunity for a fairer world. He is calling for an insurrection, but he is in no doubt as to what would be most likely to happen should the poor take matters— bread, air, life—into their own hands.

And not only the poor. In April 2020, doctors who participated in a peaceful protest against lack of PPE equipment in hospitals in Pakistan were attacked by police with AK-47 rifles, dragged through the streets, thrown into trucks and held in police detention overnight. 'I thought, how could police use violence against the frontline fighters against Covid-19 when some days ago the same officers had saluted us for leading during the pandemic?' observed one doctor. 'I was wrong.' Another doctor, who had already been forced to refuse patients due to lack of equipment—there were only nineteen ventilators in the whole region—simply commented: 'I think this pandemic is untreatable in Balochistan.'

For many of his contemporaries and critics, Camus's cry for justice, and even insurrection, did not go far enough. By the time *The Plague* was published in 1947, Camus had moved a long way from the 1930s, when he was expelled from the French Communist Party (PCF) over his support for the founder of the Algerian Popular Party, Messali Hadj. Hadj had struggled for national liberation—although not complete independence—and

was deported from Algeria as a dangerous agitator following
nationwide labour strikes and demonstrations. At that point,
Camus was seen by the PCF to be privileging the anti-colonial
struggle over the class war. There was an irony here. Camus
was an astute critic of colonialism in terms which were in many
ways ahead of his time: the 'institutional' injustice; the repeated
'lie' of assimilation; the manifest unfairness of land and income
distribution; the 'psychological suffering' and damage caused
by the 'contempt' of the colonizer towards the colonized (a critique which, as we will see, has striking affiliations with that of
Simone Weil). But, in the end, Camus would not be forgiven for
failing to back full Algerian independence, or for his later turn
against Soviet Communism as one more form of totalitarianism, a move which was seen by Jean-Paul Sartre, in their famous
falling-out, as a gift to the wrong side of the Cold War and a
betrayal of the struggle against US imperialism in Vietnam.

Before that turn, Camus was best known in France for
his role in the Resistance. He was editor of the underground
French journal *Combat*, from 1943 (a long extract of *The Plague*
appeared clandestinely in France in a collection of Resistance
publications). When it was published in full, *The Plague* was
an instant bestseller. It reprinted ten days after publication and
within a few months had sold more than fifty thousand copies.
That it was perceived as an allegory of the French Resistance
against Nazism was, for a people trying to bury national shame,
at once its strongest suit and ground for fierce critique. Simone
de Beauvoir saw the use of allegory as an evasion, since it allowed
the reader to sidestep the historical reckoning that should fall
to the French people after the stain of Vichy. The two central

characters, Rieux and Jean Tarrou, whose private chronicles of the plague Rieux draws on to tell the tale, become allies in the fight against the disease, and could fairly be described as heroes, though neither would accept the term. That epithet is reserved for the character of Joseph Grand for his acts of kindness and his dedication to an ideal (a temporary assistant municipal clerk on the 'derisory' salary of sixty-two francs and thirty centimes a day, he famously spends all his spare time writing and rewriting the first sentence of his novel). For such critics, *The Plague* was a whitewash of the inglorious part played by so many French citizens during the war. Only one character, Cottard, is recognizable as a collaborator.

At the same time, by casting the story as a chapter in the eternal moral struggle against evil, the novel laid itself open to the charge of lifting itself out of history altogether. If fascism was a scourge of nature, then no one is to blame. 'Evil sometimes has a human face,' Roland Barthes wrote in the second of two articles on the novel in 1955, 'and about this *The Plague* says nothing'. The Nazis were agents of history, not some microbe (to redirect one of the favourite Nazi metaphors for their Jewish victims). It was not enough that the allusions to the Holocaust are, as Shoshana Felman has pointed out, unmistakeable: in the hundreds of thousands of former plague victims existing in today's imagination as 'no more than a puff of smoke'; or the daily toll of ten thousand dead which, Rieux calculates, would be the equivalent of all the people crowding the exits of five crammed cinemas being led to a city square 'to die in heaps'. Nor did it seem to make any difference that the two charges seem to cancel each other out—flawed history, no history at all.

Camus felt he was being misread. The novel, he suggested, could be interpreted in three different ways: a tale about an epidemic, a symbol of Nazi occupation (and of any totalitarian regime 'no matter where'), and an exploration of the metaphysical problem of evil, as Melville had attempted in *Moby Dick*, 'with genius added'. It is not quite clear how any one of these options could be expected to satisfy the critics.

When Conor Cruise O'Brien noted the absence of Arabs from *The Plague*, he was joining a long strand of critique. Feminists would add their objection to the novel's diminished representation of women. The book opens as Rieux's wife, in search of a cure for her tuberculosis, leaves for a sanatorium in the surrounding mountains, where she will later die. His mother arrives on the day of his wife's departure, and stays with her son as the silent, self-effacing companion to a struggle in which she herself has no role to play.

In Tarrou's journals, Rieux's mother is praised for her 'effacement' and stillness, 'a motionless black figure which gradually merged into the invading darkness'. Tarrou describes the death of his own mother eight years before as her 'only effacing herself a trifle more than usual'. The women in the novel are either patient sufferers, or occasional prophetesses who are allowed to cry out their agony into the night sky. Not one of them ever attains the pitch of reflection, gifted to the male characters alone, a way of being which the novel suggests is the only true solace and ethical value to hold on to in times of plague. Rieux's mother, Tarrou tells us, 'knew everything without ever thinking'. Gilbert tries to save the day by translating 'the gift she had of knowing everything without apparently taking thought' but neither 'gift' nor 'apparently' are in the original. The women are extras, walk-off parts in relation to the male mind.

As the daily bombardment of numbers continued during Covid-19, one chilling statistic started to receive attention, the rising numbers of women who, as a consequence of lockdown, have become the victims of domestic violence with no exit, a fact which I'll return to. But imagine a scenario where your only option as a woman is to stay silently locked in the home where your life might be at risk, or travel to a place where you do not know if you will, or will not, survive. These women, we might say, have been in lockdown for a long time before the real story begins. Indeed, 'lockdown' doubles as apt description of the conditions of women in the 1940s and 1950s both inside and outside his novel, women for whom stifling domesticity was the norm. Certainly that was true for my mother, whose first two daughters, Gillian and myself, were born in 1947, the year *The Plague* was published, and 1949; her third daughter, Alison, was born in 1956. The copy of the novel I have been reading, underlined and scrawled all over with my markings, is the one I first studied for French A-level when I was seventeen.

Much, we could say, has changed—I have led a life my mother could only dream of (French A-level was in many ways where it began). But then again, perhaps not so very much. I find myself asking whether women are now in double jeopardy, subject to a form of violence which, before the crisis, they at least had a chance to escape; but perhaps also the targets of something else, a type of revenge or punishment—'backlash' as it is called—for the fact that, for most, though by no means all, women today in the Western world, being locked down, shut in, isolated in the home is no longer the norm. These women are first and foremost scapegoats for the awfulness of the hour, but they are also being murdered for their barely-won freedom. In the course of a conversation between us for the twenty-first anniversary edition of *Women, A Cultural Review*, Juliet Mitchell stated, to my complete surprise, and that of our discussant, Jean Radford, that modern-day feminism, despite its setbacks and failings, had been an unqualified success. Because, she explained, feminism will always be 'the longest revolution', the one you never give up on even in the knowledge that it is unlikely to come to an end. Reading about the women whose only option today is to be trapped in their homes with an abusive partner, it is hard to share her spirit—except perhaps in so far as the virus, just as it does in the novel, makes us newly alert to and responsible for the worst of what we see.

Who, then, is accountable for the plague? At a pivotal moment in the novel, the reader is offered one possible answer to this question by Tarrou, the chronicler on whom Rieux increasingly comes, both practically and psychologically, to rely. In their most intimate conversations, Tarrou recounts his personal story. To mark their new friendship, the two men then go for a night-time swim, using their passes as 'frontline' workers to get out on to the pier. It is the novel's unique moment of shared pleasure. 'Of course a man should fight for the victims,' Rieux comments as they agree to set off, 'but if that stops him from loving anything else, then what's the use of fighting?' They are about to undress and dive into the moonlit sea:

Before them the darkness stretched out into infinity. Rieux, who could feel under his hand the gnarled, weather-worn visage of the rocks, felt a strange happiness. Turning to Tarrou, he caught a glimpse on his friend's calm and serious face of the same happiness, a happiness that forgets nothing, not even murder.

The French is '*assassinat*', which can translate as 'murder' or 'killing'. The word comes close to the idea of calculated crime and from there to mass murder, something the world had just witnessed, which had not yet been named either as 'genocide' or as a 'crime against humanity' but soon would be.

For Tarrou, murder is state murder. His most disturbing childhood memory is watching in the courtroom as his father, a prosecuting attorney, condemned a convict to death ('His head must fall'). The convict was clearly guilty and horrified at what he had done. He looked like a 'red-haired owl blinded by too much light', tie awry, head swivelling in despair. Up to that moment, Tarrou had believed in his own innocence as a man, but from then on he realizes that to be a citizen subject is to be involved in sanctioned murder every day. No one is exempt or unscathed ('*indemne*'). Even those who are better than the rest, he explains, cannot prevent themselves from killing or letting others kill: 'Such is the logic by which they live and we can't stir a finger in this world without bringing the risk of death to somebody.' Alienated from his father, he becomes an activist for the abolition of the death penalty, but this fails to assuage his guilt. He is no less appalled at the justification of killing in the service of revolution (as indeed was Camus). The plague comes to him as no surprise: 'I had plague already,' he opens his monologue, 'long before I knew this town and this epidemic.' He is a carrier ('*un pestiféré*'), liable to infect others at every turn: 'Each of us has the plague within him; no one, no one on earth is free from it. And I know too that we must keep endless watch on ourselves lest in a careless moment we breathe in somebody's face and fasten the infection on him.' Tarrou has run social distancing into the epicentre of state power.

The proposition that we are all killers collides with 'Thou shalt not kill', perhaps the fiercest of the commandments. Tarrou is therefore very far from intoning that 'we are all miserable sinners,' the soft, handwringing lament which he has already dispatched in his exchange with Father Paneloux. Nor is he scrambling key distinctions, in the way the novel as a whole was accused. He is not conflating resistors and collaborators— Cottard is 'an accomplice' who is also in flight from some hidden past crime, Grand is a hero—or equating the powerful and destitute. All his sympathies are with the 'owl' in the dock, whatever his crime may have been. Rather he is pointing the finger at the modern state which forbids violence to its citizens, not because, as Freud puts it, 'it desires to abolish it, but because it desires to monopolize it, like salt and tobacco'. For Tarrou, the responsibility of the citizen for his own violence is not reduced by such fraudulence, but intensified, since it forces him to confront what the state enacts in his name. The plague will continue to crawl out of the woodwork—out of bedrooms, cellars, trunks, handkerchiefs and old papers—as long as human subjects do not question the cruelty and injustice of their social arrangements. We are all accountable for the ills of the world in which we live.

Tarrou aspires to be an 'innocent murderer' (even at one point to be a saint), by which he means one who recognizes the plague as his problem and fights against it with every breath that he takes. On the last page, the narrator tells his readers that he wrote the story so as to leave behind a memory of the injustice and violence undergone, and in order to state 'quite simply what we learn in a time of pestilence: that there are more things to admire in men than to despise'. Who we are and what we make of the world after the plague could go either way, for better or worse. A thought for the aftermath when there will be so much to be done.

TO DIE ONE'S OWN DEATH

Thinking with Freud
in a Time of Pandemic

I want to know why we, like upside-down sunflowers,
turn to the dark side rather than to the light.

—Rachel Berdach,
The Emperor, the Sages and Death (1938)

WHAT IS LEFT OF the inner life when the world turns more
cruel, or appears to turn more cruel, than ever before? When it
reels from inflicted blows—pandemic, war, starvation, climate
devastation or all these together—what happens to the fabric
of the mind? Is its only option defensive—to batten down the
hatches, to haul up the drawbridge (to use the common figures
of speech for a subject under assault), or simply to survive? And
does that leave room to grieve, not just for those who have been
lost, but for the shards, the broken pieces and muddled fragments of the human heart that make us who we are? Barely six
months after the outbreak of the First World War, on Christ-
mas Day 1914, Freud wrote to Ernest Jones lamenting that the

psychoanalytic movement 'is now perishing in the strife of nations' (the two men were on opposite sides in the war). 'I do not delude myself,' he wrote. 'The springtime of our science has abruptly broken off . . . all we can do is to keep the fire flickering in a few hearths, until a more favourable wind makes it possible to light it again to full blaze.' At a time of pandemic, is there room for anything like the complex reckoning with life and with death that is the unique domain of psychoanalysis?

As our screens flicker daily with the toll of the dead, it is hard not to be overcome by the scale of a tragedy that has left people we love dying in isolation, funerals pared back beyond decency, the rituals of family commemoration that make death manageable, or almost manageable, outlawed. Not to speak of the interminable counting that reduces humans to abstractions, robbing us a second time of each individual loss, even while, in the words of the British palliative care doctor Rachel Clarke, the pandemic 'unfolds one death at a time'. 'When the statistics threaten to throw me off balance,' she wrote of her struggle to restore dignity to those dying in hospital, 'I try to keep things as small as I can.'

In such moments, it is perhaps even harder to allow ourselves to admit our emotional ambivalence towards the dead as much as the living, which, in our non-pandemic existence—if such a world can be imagined again—is our daily psychic fare. Truth, they say, is the first casualty of war, but psychic truth is not what is being talked about. War and pandemic strip the mind bare. They share a brute ability to smother our psychic repertoire. Just for a second, and if only in the public mind, they make grief seem pure. We cheer soldiers off to battle and weep when they fall; we stand gut-wrenched and helpless as a pandemic ravages its way through the homes that allowed us to cherish the illusion of safety. 'You have, my poor child, seen death break into the family for the first time, or heard about it,' Freud wrote to his eldest daughter, Mathilde, when Heinrich Graf—her uncle, his brother-in-law—died suddenly in 1908, 'and perhaps shuddered at the idea that for none of us can life be made any safer.' He offered no false consolation. We do not live in a safe world. But he did insist that, for old people like him, an awareness of the inevitable end gives life its special value— Freud was about to turn fifty-two, one of several points during his life when he was convinced he would die.

On 25 January 1920, Freud's favourite daughter, Sophie Halberstadt-Freud (whom he called his 'Sunday child'), died during her third pregnancy from complications arising from Spanish flu, which had wiped out millions across Europe since the first recorded case on 4 March 1918. His daughter was one of its late casualties, falling like a soldier killed just when peace is declared—a bitter irony given that the final wave which killed her was by no means the most deadly of the three. In fact, according to some analysts, this was a fourth wave exclusive to northern countries, many of whose citizens had wrongly believed themselves to be free of the disease by December 1918, when there had been time to recover from the surge in infections following the Armistice celebrations in the streets. Beyond the fact of their historical coincidence, the plague and the war were two piled up disasters. The destiny of one was bound to the fate of the other. Erich Ludendorff, the commander of the German forces, declared that the Spanish flu had robbed him of victory. Things had started to go downhill for the Central

Powers in April 1918, when the disease made its first appearance in the trenches: until March that year they had believed they could win the war.

The Spanish flu is barely included in lists of the world's modern afflictions, even though its death toll came close to the combined toll of the two world wars. Laura Spinney—whose book about the Spanish flu, *Pale Rider*, was published a couple of years before the onset of Covid-19—suggests that what can fairly be described as the worst 'massacre' of the twentieth century has been rubbed out of history. Censorship also tracked the course of the disease, the extent of whose devastation was, just like today, silenced or palmed off from one country to the next. It was only called 'Spanish' flu because Spain—neither the country of origin nor the most stricken—was the only nation not to suppress the truth of its virulent nature. Freud himself barely mentions it, though it claimed the lives of 15,000 Viennese. By autumn 1918, schools and theatres in the city were being intermittently closed to reduce the risk of infection. In 1919, the year before Sophie's death, three of Freud's other children, Anna, Ernst and Mathilde, had fallen ill. In May that year his wife, Martha, after years of undernourishment as she tried to manage caring for the whole family through the war, went down with a case of '*grippe-pneumonie*', with recurrent waves of high fever, from which she took two months to recover.

Conditions were not alleviated at the end of the war, when a defeated Austria was left, in the words of Stefan Zweig, 'a mutilated rump, bleeding from all arteries'. By then Freud, far from his earlier, exhilarated support for the Central Powers, welcomed the dismantling of the Habsburg Empire: 'I weep not a single tear for *this* Austria or *this* Germany.' ('All my libido is given to Austro-Hungary,' he had pronounced in 1914 in response to the declaration of war.) 'We are all of us slowly failing,' he wrote to Jones in January 1919, 'in health and bulk.' By April, he wrote to Ferenczi, his family was subsisting on a 'starvation diet' ('*Hungerkost*'). A year later, Freud and his wife were unable to get to their sick daughter because there were no trains—'not even a children's train', he wrote on 27 January 1920 to the Swiss pastor Oskar Pfister, referring to the trains of the international children's association that were ferrying children out of starving Austria.

Over the preceding years, Freud's greatest anxiety had been for his sons Martin and Ernst, who had eagerly enlisted when war began (a third son, Oliver, rejected for active service, served as an army engineer). The dangers they faced at the front troubled his dreams. A nightmare in 1915 had as its manifest content 'very clearly the death of my sons, Martin first of all' (he called it a 'prophetic dream'). All his sons would outlive their father's night-time prophecy, but he was right to tremble on their behalf. Martin, a prisoner of war on the Italian front, eventually returned home in April 1919, but he was one of the lucky ones. More than a million Austro-Hungarian soldiers died either in battle or from disease. At no point did Freud have the slightest intimation—why would he?—that it was the fate of his daughter at the mercy of the Spanish flu which he should most dread.

It was in response to Covid-19 that the date of the Freud Memorial lecture on which this chapter is based had to be moved from 6 May, the anniversary of Freud's birth, to 23 September, the anniversary of the day he died in 1939—a switch which echoed the tension between affirmation and destruction, between life and death, that from 1919 onwards was increasingly at the core of Freud's work. It was no doubt in response to this pressing context that I found myself newly alert to the wretchedness of the hour as it closed around Freud's family in Vienna—around the walls of what is now the Freud Museum where I should have been speaking—first during the First World War and its aftermath, and then on the cusp of the even more deadly Second World War. I became acutely aware, that is, of the way the disasters of history penetrate, float in and out, ricochet and are repudiated by the mind—including my own since, during a lifelong preoccupation with Freud, I had not fully grasped the scope of this reality before.

Psychoanalysis begins with a mind in flight, a mind that cannot take the measure of its own pain. It begins, that is, with the recognition that the world—or what Freud sometimes referred to as 'civilization'—makes demands on human subjects that are too much to bear. Rereading the famous biographies—Jones, Peter Gay, Max Schur—I was now struck by just how exposed and vulnerable Freud was to the ills, major and petty, of the times, and by the fierce contrasts in his moods between blindness and insight, equanimity and dismay. Freud was articulate about what he personally found most insufferable: debt was his greatest fear (by the end of the war he had lost 95 per cent of his cash savings); to those afflicted by poverty he responded with a mix of compassion and dread; he hated rationing; there were no lengths he would not go to in order to secure the precious cigars that were killing him. For all the privilege of this Viennese family, they skirted penury and floundered in wellbeing and health. As we have recently seen only too clearly, disaster uncovers the material and racial fault-lines of a society, but it also unforgivingly exposes the truth that no human subject is spared, in Freud's words, 'the perplexity and helplessness of the human race'.

To read Freud against this backdrop is to observe someone capable of the wildest fluctuations, covering the entire range of moods to which everyone I know, affected by today's pandemic, has at one point or another succumbed. 'We are suffering under no restrictions, no epidemic, and are in good spirits,' he wrote to Jones at the start of the war, before his misplaced faith in the cause of the Central Powers began to wane. 'Curiously,' he wrote to the Hungarian psychoanalyst Sándor Ferenczi in February 1917 (when food was scarce and lack of heating froze his fingers, making anything apart from letter-writing impossible), 'my spirits are unshaken'—'proof', he continued, of 'how little justification in reality one needs for inner wellbeing'. In August 1918 he wrote to Karl Abraham to say that he could once again venture to 'join in the world's pleasure and the world's pain'. He was citing Goethe, although the German word '*tragen*' is less 'join in' than 'bear' or 'endure' ('*der Erde Lust, der Erde Leid zu tragen*'), as if in the world he was living, pleasure, no less than pain, had become a burden.

He would also plunge into mental darkness. 'One has to use every means possible to withdraw from the frightful tension in the world outside,' he wrote to Ferenczi in 1916. 'It is not to be borne.' In November 1914, as the full horror of the war was beginning to emerge, he wrote to Lou Andreas-Salomé: 'I and my contemporaries will never again see a joyous world. It is too hideous.' Mankind was a doomed experiment and did not deserve to survive. 'We have to abdicate,' he continued, 'and the Great Unknown, he or it, lurking behind Fate, will one day repeat such an experiment with another race.' In an extraordinary gesture of radical self-abnegation—not the type of gesture for which he is best known—Freud was willing to sacrifice humanity, as we might say these days, to save the planet (he could not of course have foreseen today's Voluntary Human Extinction Movement whose motto is 'May we live long and die out'). Later, in the 1930s, with the next war on the horizon, he again speculated that the human race was approaching its end, now that the 'perfection of the instruments of destruction' allowed two enemies to exterminate each other. Our great failing, he suggested, was the gulf which 'earlier periods of human arrogance had torn too wide apart between mankind and the animals'. Freud's despair was global and multi-species in its reach (a fact that seems to have received virtually no commentary, given the common travesty that his concerns were restricted to the small, privileged elite of Vienna). But it was the tragedy closer to home, Sophie's death, that ushered his grief into a new phase—though it would not be until the death from tuberculosis of his grandson Heinele, Sophie's second child, three years later, at the age of four, that he would declare all his joy in the world gone for ever. 'I myself was aware,' he wrote to his Hungarian friends Katà and Lajos Lévy, 'of never having loved a human being, certainly never a child, so much.' Years later he would write to his friend Ludwig Binswanger, after Binswanger's son had died: 'We shall remain inconsolable and never find a substitute. . . . It is the only way of perpetuating the love which we do not wish to renounce'—an idea that could not be further from his best-known writing on mourning as a task to be completed.

So what, on the hundredth anniversary of the death of Sophie Halberstadt-Freud, did the loss of the daughter do to her father, Sigmund Freud? And how might this story help us confront the awfulness of our own time, when unimaginable deaths—Freud described the war as 'inconceivable'—are again legion? In 1924, Fritz Wittels, Freud's first biographer, suggested that there was a link between Sophie's death and *Beyond the Pleasure Principle* (1920), in which Freud introduced the idea of the death drive. Freud's rebuttal came fast. The suggestion was implausible, he said. He wrote the first draft in 1919, when Sophie was still alive. It turns out that Freud had pre-empted Wittels; in July 1920, four years before the biography appeared, he had written to Max Eitingon: 'You will be able to certify that it was half-finished when Sophie was alive and flourishing.' This is already bizarre—'half-finished' leaves plenty of room for additions after her death. Why, we might ask, would the fact that it was completed before she died be presented as something which, in an unspecified future, would need to be *certified* ('*sie werden bestätigen können*')? Today, thanks to the indefatigable efforts of the Freud scholar Ilse Grubrich-Simitis, who first brought the early manuscripts of his writing to light, we know that he was being evasive (she describes these 'hitherto neglected and silent' documents as 'rough-hewn and overwhelming'). An entirely new sixth chapter, the longest by far, was added to a later draft, making up almost a third of the published text. The new chapter contained the first appearance in print of the term 'death drive'. Its only earlier appearance was in two letters to Eitingon of February 1920, just weeks after Sophie's death. I think it would, therefore, be fair to say that Freud owes the genesis of this unprecedented concept to her.

In his response to Wittels, Freud is dismissive—the word Grubrich-Simitis uses is 'laconic'—acknowledging only a single addition to the text: a 'discussion concerning the mortality or immortality of protozoa'. He surely displays here what he called the 'kettle logic' of the unconscious, in which a defendant offers a run of arguments, each invalidating the next: he had finished the text already; there is nothing significant in the additions he made; the only new material concerned the immortality and/or mortality of biological life (as if such a topic could have no bearing on the death of a child). In his letter to Pfister after Sophie died, he described her as being 'snatched away . . . as if she had never been'. 'The undisguised brutality of our time,' he continued, 'weighs heavily on us.' Nothing, surely, conveys the pain of a life being snuffed out forever more than loved ones in the prime of their lives dying in the midst of a war or pandemic (in this historic moment of Freud's life, both more or less at the same time). How do you hold on to any intimation of futurity beyond death—whether in the shape of the immortal germ plasm or the eternal soul—when people all around you are dying like flies?

Beyond the Pleasure Principle is one of the most important works of the second half of Freud's life. It is the culmination of his thinking on the topography of the mind and it introduces the new dualism of the drives (it was also the first of his works to be published as an individual monograph). It has excited passionate enthusiasm and virulent hostility in equal measure. In his biography of Freud, Max Schur goes to considerable lengths to discredit it, which may seem odd given that his own book is devoted to understanding the place of death in Freud's life and work. But the idea of an unconscious demonic principle driving the psyche to distraction could be said to sabotage once and for all the vision of man in control of his mind—and for Schur, as for many others, it was therefore anathema.

I am not exaggerating. Schur was Freud's physician in his dying years. When the pain of Freud's cancer left his life without value or meaning, Schur—on the basis of a spoken agreement between them—administered the fatal dose of morphine. It was unquestionably Freud's wish, and Schur is eloquent on the dignity with which he approached the end of his life after sixteen years of suffering. But at the risk of wild analysis—analysis outside the consulting room—my reading is that Schur could only live with what he had done so long as he could trust in man's ability to subordinate his will to his reason, and—contrary, one might say, to the entire spirit of psychoanalysis—always to do what is best for himself.

Who does death belong to? If this has become a question during today's pandemic it is because the lack of state provision, the missing medical supplies, the dearth of equipment and isolation from human touch have made it feel to many for the first time that death is something of which a person—the one dying, and those closest to her or him—can be robbed. Freud and his wife could not reach their sick daughter because there was no transport, not even the trains getting children out of a starving country in the aftermath of war. They could not be with her when she died. This may help us to understand these remarkable lines from *Beyond the Pleasure Principle*, from what we now know to be its new sixth chapter: 'If we are to die ourselves, and first to lose in death those who are dearest to us, it is easier to submit to a remorseless law of nature, to the sublime ἀνάγκη [necessity], than to a chance that might perhaps have been escaped.' In the preceding chapter, Freud had been elaborating on the repetition compulsion, which he had first identified in soldiers returning from battle who found themselves reliving their worst experiences in night-time and waking dreams. Slowly tracing this tendency from the front to the consulting room (patients wedded to their symptoms), Freud concludes that such a compulsion is a property of all living matter. The urge of all organic life is to restore an earlier state of things. What follows is a considerable downgrade in the status of the drives of self-preservation and mastery that were key to his earlier topography of the mind, as they are all now seen to be working in the service of the organism's need to follow the path to its own death: 'The organism wishes to die only in its own fashion.' 'The aim of all life,' Freud states in perhaps one of his most counterintuitive affirmations, 'is death.'

In this theoretical trajectory—by Freud's own account one of his most speculative—he is moving between elegy and treatise, between sorrow and science: 'We are strengthened in our belief,' he says, 'by the writings of our poets.' But what stood out here for me this time was a dimension that seemed to enter his thought with the death of Sophie, to which we can now confidently say this whole chapter came in response. Better death as a silent companion than a death that falls out of the skies. A remorseless law of nature is preferable to a death that should—might—not have taken place. The resonance during the Covid-19 pandemic could not be more striking, as one person after another is confronted with the intolerable idea that their loved ones died through the sheer, reckless inefficiency of political scoundrels whose behaviour, in the words of one *Guardian* newspaper columnist, 'is often indistinguishable from deliberate destructiveness'.

We know that all Freud's writing coils out of his inner world, but I can think of no other moment when he lays his psychological cards on the table with such transparency. Nothing worse than the idea of death as part of a string of accidents. Hence the numerous cases of negligence which are being brought against the UK government on behalf of some of the twenty thousand victims of Covid-19 who, if lockdown had been declared one week earlier in March 2020, would not have died: care workers in their twenties, young, predominantly BIPOC nurses and doctors, dementia sufferers who, once their families could no longer visit, lost the will to live. Through the merciless nature of their deaths, the victims of pandemic and war are being deprived of the essence of life. This is what Freud is trying to give back to his daughter, restoring her rightful inheritance. To put it simply: without the belief that life should move along its path to its own end, her sudden death—five days after falling ill—would have been too much for him to bear: 'easier to submit to a remorseless law of nature . . . than to a chance that might perhaps have been escaped'. 'Perhaps,' he adds, 'we have adopted the belief because there is some comfort in it.' 'It may be,' he adds, citing Schiller, 'that this belief in the internal necessity of dying is only another of those illusions which we have created "*um die Schwere das Daseins zu ertragen*" ["to bear the burden of existence"].' He was warding off her destiny, naming it for the outrage it was. Today, for all the glaring differences of class and race in how, where and whom the pandemic strikes, this prospect of sudden and random death has to include just about everyone. Freud is offering a philosophy of grief. He helps us understand why what is happening among us now can feel as much an internal as an external catastrophe. Death in a pandemic is no way to die.

Freud's dismissal, in his exchange with Wittels, of his own ruminations on the immortality of the germ plasm should give us pause. As if immortality were not something you were likely to find yourself thinking about after the death of a child. This perhaps partly explains the reason why, in a letter to Ferenczi written two weeks after Sophie died, grief-stricken as he was, he described her loss as a 'narcissistic injury', to be uncovered deep beneath the daily duties through which he was finding his way back into his life. 'I do as much work as I can,' he had written to Pfister two days after she died, 'and am grateful for the distraction. The loss of a child seems to be a grave blow to one's narcissism.'

A closer look at Chapter Six of *Beyond the Pleasure Principle*, which sees Freud on the trail of biological death, can perhaps guide us here (although, as he notes, in the writing of biologists, the whole concept of death 'melts away in their hands'). His question is whether biology will confirm his conviction that death is an inherent property of all organic life, or whether there is something in living substance that is immortal. According to the evolutionary biologist August Weismann, death belongs solely to multicellular organisms whose soma dies at the moment of reproduction when the germ plasm enters a new living form. Unicellular organisms, on the other hand, do not appear to die but eternally reproduce themselves. Or you could argue, as Max Hartmann did in *Death and Reproduction* (1906), that death cannot be reduced to the appearance of a dead body, but describes the moment when a cell comes to the end of its individual development as it mutates and gives itself over to the next stage of life.

What matters here is not whether biology can actually give backing to Freud's troubled concept of a human drive to death. As is so often the case in his work, the issue is what these preoccupations generate, what they allow him to go on thinking about. 'In this sense,' Freud writes with more than a hint of satisfaction, 'protozoa too are mortal; in their case death always coincides with reproduction, but it is to some extent obscured by it, since the whole substance of the parent animal may be transmitted directly into the young offspring.' The only thing that saves the organism from dying is its passage, entire, into its offspring—perish the thought, one might say. Transpose this into human life, and the death of a biological child becomes a narcissistic injury because it is only through the existence of children that the parent has a stab at eternity. What Freud is saying here is as chilling as it is simple. The only thing that keeps a parent alive is their child.

Freud's death drive seems, therefore, to lose itself in the minutiae of organic life. But at the same time it reaches into the external political world: contrary to what is often suggested, the two realms of Freud's thinking work in tandem. Remember that the war was the essential backdrop to the concept of the repetition compulsion as returning soldiers were reliving the dangers inflicted by the outside world (the very concept of trauma which, according to an influential misreading, Freud—from the 1890s onwards—had definitively left behind). Freud's preoccupation with organic life and with the perils of the world, with inmost biological process and external hardship, become increasingly tied up in his thought, just as the question of what we inherit without knowing it (our predisposition), and what the world rains down on us (the accidents of life) begin to come together on the same page. I have no doubt that it is Covid-19 that has newly alerted me to these strange alliances, not least as I struggle, like so many, to bring into some psychic alignment the pain of my inner life and the tragedy unfolding outside my door.

How to link these domains becomes the preoccupation of the second phase of Freud's working life. This is what war does to theory. At a symposium on 'The Psychoanalysis of the War Neuroses', delivered at the Fifth International Psychoanalytical Congress held in Budapest in 1918, Freud refuses the distinction between war neuroses and peacetime neuroses, which pits the external threat of the former against the internal libidinal conflict of the latter. Freud wants to unite them. The difficulties in doing so, he concludes, cease to be insuperable if one 'described repression, which lies at the basis of every neurosis, as a reaction to a trauma—*as an elementary traumatic neurosis*'. Repression, which is the foundation of all neuroses, is a trauma in and of itself. No one escapes. In the midst of the war, trauma, we might say, has been reinstated, straddling the division between inner

and outer worlds. By his own account, a traumatized soldier is
torn between the two: between the demands of loyalty to his
ego—which tells him to avoid danger at any cost—and loyalty
to his nation, which requires that he be prepared to die.

Are war and pandemic the worst things that can happen to humankind? If at first sight this seems an insane question—though
not, as we will see, as insane as Freud's reply—it nonetheless
has resonance for the task he has set for himself of trying to
track the impact of the world on its subjects, and of bygone
ages on present time. We have seen that a preoccupation with
immortality, duration and transmission runs through Chapter
Six of *Beyond the Pleasure Principle*, as Freud tried to navigate
his daughter's death and face up to the fact that a link in the
chain of being had been broken beyond repair. But in another
work written in the middle of the war, Freud follows a different
path of prehistory. This time it is not the life of the germ plasm
but a far-off epoch when existence could fairly be described
as hell on earth—war and pandemic shrink by its side. I am
referring to Freud's twelfth meta-psychological paper, which
he did not wish to see the light of day, and which none of us
would have been able to access without the scholarly devotion
of Grubrich-Simitis, who published it in 1987 under the title 'A
Phylogenetic Fantasy'. It was one of seven meta-psychological
papers that Freud discarded or destroyed. Retrieving it against his
wishes, Grubrich-Simitis was playing Max Brod to his Kafka. She
calls it a 'document of failure'—it is truly wild—but also accords

it the deepest respect, arguing that it is the text in which Freud's theories of the drive and of trauma, so often seen as incompatible, reveal their deepest affiliation. 'My thesis,' she writes, 'is that Freud, in his phylogenetic fantasy, once again made an effort to integrate theoretically the traumatic aspects of pathogenesis into the drive model—a task with which we are still confronted today.'

'The Phylogenetic Fantasy', or 'Overview of the Transference Neuroses', makes the speculations of *Beyond the Pleasure Principle* look like hard science. In the beginning, Freud narrates, an Ice Age turned man into an anxious animal when 'the hitherto predominantly friendly outside world . . . transformed itself into a mass of threatening perils'. 'Food was not sufficient to permit an increase in the human hordes, and the powers of the individual were not enough to keep so many helpless beings alive.' Faced with an emergency 'beyond his control', man imposed on himself a ban on reproduction, since to propagate the species in a time of such want was to put his very existence on the line: no children, no future, no glimpse of eternal life. Man's response to such a brute curtailing of his drives was hysteria: the origins of conversion hysteria in modern times where the libido is a danger to be subdued. Man also became a tyrant, bestowing on himself unrestrained dominance as a reward for his power to safeguard the lives of the many: 'Language was magic to him, his thoughts seemed omnipotent to him, he understood the world according to his ego.' I love this. Tyranny is the silent companion of catastrophe, as has been so flagrantly demonstrated in the behaviour of the rulers of several nations across the world today, not least Donald Trump in his response to Covid-19. As if to say: I will save you, but you must make me king (not that such rulers save anyone). Not to mention the accompanying idea that the tyrant was the first hysteric: the idea of bodily panic as the unspoken subtext of masculine power is as unexpected—and as progressive—as any of Freud's thoughts. Note how political he is being in a text too easily dismissed as sheer fantasy, including by Freud himself. Rather, I suggest that we see this paper as a thought experiment allowing him to take huge, and unprecedented, mental strides.

What passes through the generations, then, deep within the psyche of the people, is anxiety. Anxiety in response to an imperilled world, but also as a reaction to the tyranny of the powers that come to meet it. This is what children usher down through the generations: 'The children bring along the anxiousness of the beginning of the Ice Age.' The child is repeating the history of the species, offering Freud support in his belief in phylogenetic transmission—the 'preponderance of the phylogenetic disposition over all other factors'. A year later, in Lecture 23 of the *Introductory Lectures on Psychoanalysis*, 'The Path to Symptom Formation', he states, 'I have repeatedly been led to suspect that the psychology of the neuroses has stored up in it more of the antiquities of human development than any other source.' (In *Totem and Taboo*, he had suggested that guilt can be stored in the unconscious of peoples for 'many thousands of years.') 'What,' he asks, 'are the ways and means employed by one generation in order to hand on its mental states to the next one?' An emphasis which, he also insists, does not eliminate the question of acquisition: 'It only moves it into still earlier prehistory.' This is Freud's Lamarckism, to which he remained committed, even when Lamarck's findings had been scientif-ically discredited (although whether this is in fact the case is contested by genetic theorists today).

What this strange unpublished meditation reveals is that the concept of phylogenesis, far from being some biologistic remnant in his thought, is his way of acknowledging the parlous state of mankind: want, poverty, affliction and trouble, the catastrophes of history, the burden of the past. Modern-day psychoanalysis talks of 'transgenerational haunting', the unconscious passage of historical trauma from one generation to the next. We bring our ancestors behind us, which means that, while we may die our own death, we also die on behalf of others who were there before us. Once more ahead of his time, Freud took this reality, which is now clinically recognized, and injected it into the bloodstream of humankind. The organism passes its entire substance into the next generation. Freud's 1915 paper reminds us of the price of living in a world of disaster. As Grubrich-Simitis put it in a 1987 lecture on the topic, Freud was writing a guide for what was to come 'should we want to imagine a new man-made Ice Age, and think in psychoanalytic terms about the consequences of a nu-clear winter'. Nuclear winter then, pandemic or climate catastro-phe now: the document still has no less, and no less alarming, resonance.

We are not done with the death drive. My attempt to grap-ple with it would be deeply misleading if I stopped there. In Freud's account, that drive does not only belong on the side of quiescence, the slow, steady return of the living organism to an inanimate state. If the death drive is one of the most controver-sial of Freud's theories, it is not just because of the deathly pallor it casts over life. It is also—perhaps even more so—because it turns violence into the internal property of everyone. This aspect of the drive proved to be an idea even more scandalous than Freud's earlier belief that the drive for pleasure was the chief motivator of human life. Not least because it put paid to the cherished illusion that the evils of the world are the responsibility of everyone other than oneself. In 1929, Freud wrote to Einstein:

> All our attention is directed to the outside, whence dangers threaten and satisfactions beckon. From the inside, we only want to be left in peace. So if someone tries to turn our attention inward, in effect twisting its neck, then our whole organization resists—just as, for example, the oesophagus and the urethra resist any attempt to reverse their normal direction of passage.

This must be one of his most visceral statements on the reason for the public hostility toward psychoanalysis. 'There is nothing for which man's capabilities are less suited,' he had written somewhat more decorously to Binswanger in 1911, 'than psychoanalysis.'

Once again, this idea, elaborated for the first time in Chapter Six of *Beyond the Pleasure Principle*, is deeply imbricated in war. We may conjecture that it would have made Freud's task too easy, his own grief fraudulent, if he had not also considered the way war shatters the innocence of the human mind—after all, to begin with, all his libido had been on the side of the war. What drives people crazy in wartime is their capacity, after a lifetime of prohibition and restraint, to take violence upon themselves. Not just because killing presents man with a clash, as Freud puts it, between 'the claims of humanity' and 'the demands of a national war'. But because it brings him up against the violence that is an inner portion of being human. 'Consider,' Freud wrote in his 1916 introductory lecture on the censorship of dreams,

> the Great War which is still laying Europe waste. Think of the vast amount of brutality, cruelty and lies which are able to spread over the civilized world. Do you really believe that a handful of ambitious and deluding men without conscience could have succeeded in unleashing all these evil spirits if their millions of followers did not share their guilt?

As in 1916, so in 2016 with the election of Trump, and since, in the era of Bolsonaro, Modi, Erdoğan, Orbán, Duterte et al. 'We lay a stronger emphasis on what is evil in men,' he continued, 'only because other people disavow it, and thereby make the human mind, not better, but incomprehensible.'

I began by suggesting that one thing which today's pandemic is depriving us of is the ambivalence of human grief. But as I was writing it came to seem unsurprising to me that Freud should emerge in these pages as a thinker of disaster. In a world today gone numb under the pressure of incompetence, lies and false triumphalism, his ideas can help us restore, first the bald truth of what is happening, and then—and only on that basis—all the shades of our inner world that live and die in the unconscious. In a relatively unknown section of *Thoughts for the Times on War and Death*, written in 1915, Freud describes the birth pangs of ethical life arising when man, as yet unsullied by civilization, confronted the mix of emotions—despair, rage, hatred and pleasure—that he experienced in the face of death, especially towards those he loved most. 'In each of the loved persons,' he writes, 'there was also something of the stranger . . . there adheres to the tenderest and most intimate of our love-relations a small portion of hostility which can excite an unconscious death-wish.' Out of this mix arises the first ethical commandment, 'Thou shalt not kill': 'It was acquired,' he writes, 'in relation to dead people who were loved as a reaction against the satisfaction hidden behind the grief for them; and it was gradually extended to strangers who were not loved, and finally even to enemies.' But, he observes, with an eye to the unfolding war, such an embrace of everyone, enemies included, has been lost to so-called 'civilized man', together with the 'vein of ethical sensitiveness' that accompanied it.

When teaching Freud, I use these lines to convey to students that, at decisive moments, he was far less ethnocentric than is often assumed. But what makes these thoughts so relevant today is the implied message, one that is barely audible at a time when the exile of the psyche to the outskirts of existence—like death in the time of Walter Benjamin—is the unshared secret of the hour. Only if you admit your ambivalence even towards those you love most is there the faintest chance that you will reach out across the world to everyone, including your putative enemies: to China, for example, a country the Western world is now being told to hate; to black men being mown down on the streets; to the citizens of another country which, in the race for a Covid-19 vaccine, may just be ahead in the game; to all those who are also suffering, whether from war or pandemic, or, like everyone else, simply from the fact of being human. But for this to happen, the present-day run of narcissistic—mainly male—leaders would first have to acknowledge their failings, something of which they seem constitutionally incapable, and then, as a consequence, withdraw their casually dispersed and carefully targeted hatreds. 'I, of course, belong to a race,' Freud wrote to Romain Rolland in 1923, 'which in the Middle Ages was held responsible for all epidemics.' Ten years later, in a letter to Marie Bonaparte, he predicted that persecution of the Jews and the suppression of intellectual freedom were the only parts of Hitler's project that were likely to succeed. He would have been appalled, we can safely assume, by the blame-game, not to speak of the increasingly vicious targeting of refugees, which has become the daily accompaniment to Covid-19.

Although Freud remarked that the impulse to human empathy is difficult to explain, that compassion can be a veil for narcissism, there are moments in his writing, again in *Beyond the Pleasure Principle*, when the bare outlines of such an impulse can be found: the protective shield of the psyche which allows itself to die to save the deeper layers of the mind from a similar fate; or the community of cells which survive even if individual cells have to die. Something is working through Freud's text, a 'socius primitive' in Jacques Derrida's reading, or a new form of common life which sheds the pitfalls of the singular ego. Or, to permit a modern-day example, like black activist Patrick Hutchinson carrying a far-right protestor to safety, at the risk of his own, in the midst of the Black Lives Matter demonstrations in London of June 2020. The video clip went viral for what it made momentarily seem possible. A life in which the pain of the times is shared, and in which every human subject, regardless of race, class, caste or sex would be able to participate. This may be what it means to struggle for a world in which everyone is free to die their own death.

To end with two writers I have only recently encountered, both of whose lives brushed against Freud's and who, in their different ways, bring these issues into stark relief. The first is Rachel Berdach, who got in touch with Freud in 1938, shortly after he arrived in London 'to die in freedom'. Both Berdach and Freud had escaped from the Nazis; four of Freud's five sisters who had remained were deported to Theresienstadt; one died in the ghetto, the other three in the Treblinka extermination camp. Berdach had sent him her novel, *The Emperor, the Sages and Death*—a 'mysterious and beautiful book', he wrote to her, which 'pleased me so much it made me unsure of my judgement'. 'Who are you?' Freud asked. 'Where did you acquire all the knowledge expressed in your book?' He invited her to meet him, and assumed, although this may sound counterintuitive, that given the priority her novel grants to death, she must be very young. Schur notes that the meeting between them took place though there appears to be no detailed record (it was one of the final encounters of his life). As for her age, Freud was right and wrong. In 1938 she was 60 years old; Freud was 82. But according to Theodor Reik, who had been her analyst, she had composed the novel in her head as a young woman, reciting it to herself word by word over decades, unwilling to commit it to print because of a fear that had set in following the death of someone she had loved. It was only after the far greater losses she experienced at the hands of the Nazis that she had been finally able to commit her novel to writing.

The book would merit an entire essay to itself. It is orchestrated as a set of philosophical dialogues between the thirteenth-century German emperor and enlightened despot Frederick II, the Egyptian Arab physician Abu Sina and the rabbi Jacob Charif ben Aron. There are also several Catholic anti-Semites. Across the borders of race and creed, the novel stages a meeting and clashing of minds. The psychoanalytic resonances are everywhere, from the emperor's wish to understand man's propensity for the dark (the epigraph to this chapter), to the rabbi's description of Jewish understanding as aimed not just at what is being kept secret but at what is unknown. As Freud observes, this is a novel about dying. 'I wish to be conscious to the very end,' the emperor asserts, 'so as not to lose life's most mysterious part.' When the rabbi's scribe, Michael Ben Chacham, dies, the rabbi finds in his desk a batch of papers held together by parchment, which include these despairing lines: 'Is man alone accursed to know of death while full with life?' Do leaves fear autumn's 'deathly winds'? Do fruits long for the tree from which they fall? Do beasts hear death's 'approaching steps'? 'How come,' he exclaims, 'we don't love each other? Do we not share one fate?'

Again, this knowledge has the profoundest social and cultural repercussions. Death is, or should be, the great equalizer, flattening out the arbitrary distinctions between us. This is the rabbi's cherished vision, whose political implications rebound in our time. His most fervent wish is to be neither ruler nor slave: 'My dream is this: not to be ruler in my land, in any land, neither be slave in any place, not to erect new boundaries—remove the old ones for all, not to be chosen . . . My Canaan is the soil that all men plough.' For a Jew to express such sentiments—not to be chosen, Canaan as the land for all men to plough—is close to blasphemy, especially in the historical context of what was in 1938 the ongoing struggle over Palestine. What is this glimpse of an alternative ethical life? In a key chapter, the characters light on a doll's house in the imperial library which has inscribed over the gate: 'Whomever thou meetest, it is Thou.' 'What a small world, indeed,' Frederick exclaims, 'A German elector dreams he meets himself; a Jew from Spain writes the same words which, when in India, a fakir did recite for me when asked about his faith . . . *Tat twam asi*—it's you.' A bit like the Freudian unconscious, this is a world that is both one and infinite, in which everything and everybody is included, and from which nothing can escape or disappear.

But as we know, to die one's own death is not the same thing as to die alone in a world that seems deserted. In the very last pages, the rabbi wakes up one morning in a still, grey, empty world of disaster: 'Cold fear now filled his heart. Where were the people, and was there war in the town? Had they chased out the citizens or had they fled? Had they perchance been killed? Was he the only one to have been forgotten?' 'Where is he now? He cannot tell.' Slowly, realizing that something awful has happened, he is overwhelmed by a single desire, to catch up with those he is sure are about to be confronted by 'unexpected terror': 'Must he not share their fate before he dies?' He is too late. Men, beasts and plants are gone; death has swallowed the earth. Not a million miles from Grubrich-Simitis's nuclear winter or from the catastrophe of climate change, this could be a chronicle of deaths foretold for the era we are living in now. The rabbi dies in isolation, but it is to a solidarity of people amid disaster—'Must he not share their fate?'—that he commits his last breath.

In 1937, a year before the encounter between Berdach and Freud, the German psychoanalyst and neurologist John Rittmeister returned from Switzerland to Germany to complete his training analysis—at considerable risk, since he was known to the authorities for his communist sympathies. Appointed director of the Göring Institute, the skeleton psychoanalytic institute, purged of Jews, that was permitted to function under Hitler, he worked for the resistance until he was arrested by the Gestapo for treason in 1942 and executed in Plötzensee Prison in 1943. His remarkable prison diaries contain two entries that go to the heart of my theme. In the first, dated 24 December 1942, Rittmeister refers to his 'abominable fate', and then immediately chastises himself:

> I say "my abominable fate", forgetting too quickly the millions of "abominable fates" being played out across Europe and everywhere without an end to blood, suffering, tears and fear. Like someone who loses all taste because their neighbour's plate is empty, this suffering prevents me from enjoying the pleasures of life.

In the second, dated 12 January 1943, he is musing on two different ways of ethical being in the world. One is dominated by the self, where an individual simply absorbs the other into their own mental sphere, turning them into no more than an occasion for enlarging their own ego. The second path, by contrast, grants autonomy to the other—setting them free to subsist in their own way. This way of being belongs, he writes, at the core of Freud's work, which teaches us 'love, not introversion'.

Against the odds, Rittmeister was dying his own death. But how, we may ask, could a man on the brink of execution by the Nazis find room to think of the millions of others doomed to an abominable fate, and remain so expansive and open? Today, as a consequence of the pandemic, there are calls for new forms of solidarity in life and in death, and for a new inclusive, political consciousness. How, though, to find a place in this new reality for the darker aspects of being human which, like upside-down sunflowers, remain at the centre of the unfinished project of psychoanalysis? Failing which, with the best will in the world, any move we make in that direction will, I fear, prove in the long run to be an empty gesture. To make sure this does not happen, we could perhaps do worse, as I have tried to do here, than to return to Freud's radical, all-encompassing and finally loving vision.

LIVING DEATH

WHAT EXACTLY WAS BEING asked of people when they were told to 'stay at home' or 'self-isolate' in response to the first threat of Covid-19? In a BBC *Panorama* report on women who had managed to escape their abusers during lockdown, broadcast in the first year of the pandemic, one woman was asked, 'What did the "stay at home" message mean to you?' 'Death,' she replied almost inaudibly, and then repeated the word as if not expecting to be heard. Her partner damaged her internally, she said, and burned her with cigarettes 'so no one would want me'. He also never left her alone in a room: she was isolated, yet never by herself; cut off from most human contact and at the same time deprived of privacy, robbed of the capacity to find a way through her own thoughts. This is isolation without interiority, solitude leeched of its inner dimension, loneliness without redress. It leaves you with no one to turn to, including yourself. The 'self' in 'self-isolate' is therefore a decoy. It forgets all those situations—incarceration, torture—where isolation is something that one person (with the power) inflicts on another. Above all, it leaves no room to ask what happens, during a time of collective trauma, to the mind's innermost relationship to itself.

No less misleading, or at least dangerously partial, was the mantra, at the centre of lockdown policies worldwide, that staying at home will save lives (or, in one sinister government ad widely circulated on Facebook, 'If you go out, you can spread it. People will die'). Without consideration of whether staying home is possible, or what might follow when it is, this turns the body into a lethal weapon outside the sacred precincts of the home. The formula is an avatar for privilege and injustice. What are the advantages of staying indoors for a family crowded into an airless slum? Or for the low-paid workers living in cramped conditions as a result of the rising, pandemic-fuelled demand for cheap factory-produced food? Against decades of feminist argument, the phrase also made the fatal error of suggesting that the moment you reach your front door, you are safe. In the United States, women were prevented by their abusers from washing their hands so that, even in isolation (especially in isolation), their fear of infection would increase. In England, one couple sat listening to Boris Johnson on the radio when he announced the lockdown. 'He looked over at me,' the woman later described her husband, 'he had his arms folded and his chest out, 'cause he knew that would intimidate me, and he said, "Let the games begin."' He then raped her in a space invisible and inaudible to the world outside: curtains closed, front door locked, TV and music both turned up so loud that no one could hear her screaming 'for someone, for anybody'. This is isolation at degree zero, trampling over the relics of what, not so long ago—though it has felt like the distant past—was meant, for some at least, to have been a relatively safe world, a time when women in many countries, though not all women, were more or less free to walk out the door. Neither health benefit nor saving grace, the official guidance proved itself to be the hidden accomplice of cruelty, a spur to violent gender-based crime.

Slowly these stories came to light. The problem has been global—the 'shadow pandemic', in the words of a United Nations report—yet for some reason it did not seem to have crossed the minds of those in government that lockdown would be a nightmare for women trapped in abusive relationships (though I am not sure why this should come as any surprise). Visits to the website of Refuge, the United Kingdom's largest domestic-abuse charity, increased during the pandemic by over 60 per cent. True, there was a clause in the UK Coronavirus Act of April 2020—intended, we were subsequently told, for women abused in their homes—allowing that not everyone would be able to self-isolate. But the only person who seems to have made use of that clause was Boris Johnson's unelected chief adviser, Dominic Cummings, to excuse his breaking lockdown rules when—infected with Covid-19—he travelled with his family to stay with his parents in Durham. By doing so, he smashed any remaining confidence in government policies, putting thousands at risk (Cummings' subsequent sacking by Johnson had nothing to do with his infraction of the rules—on this, Johnson himself would turn out to have excelled him by miles). Britain has shared with the United States one of the highest infection and death rates in the world.

It took nineteen days after the lockdown began for funds to be released to women's refuges, which were desperately straitened after years of government austerity policies. According to the 'Counting Dead Women' campaign, during that time, sixteen women were murdered, or suspected to have been murdered by their partners—more than double the average number for such killings during an equivalent period before the pandemic. 'If you think it was bad before,' the husband said, 'you are in for a rough ride.' ('Let the games begin.') Lockdown had emboldened him, giving him a new lease on life and on death. Another woman, pregnant, was force-fed—it started as a game, almost like a fetish, she said. Her partner boasted that he didn't have to 'cover up' any more while repeatedly assuring her that she was safe at home (he would not let her leave the house to attend a hospital pregnancy scan). Another woman, Annie (not her real name), had endured two years of domestic abuse when the restrictions were imposed: 'It was at this moment she finally started to believe her partner would kill her.' Abuse in a time of pandemic—angry men walking into shuttered rooms with 'guns' blazing and a soft voice. Or, as one poster plastered across London put it, 'Abusers always work from home.'

We have been faced with a new 'femicide', the term originally coined by Diana Russell in 1976, something which the pandemic has brought out of the dark. With reference to Covid-19, Julia Kristeva uses the term 'feminicide', since it is women's presumed 'femininity' that is at stake. There is, Kristeva suggests, a central 'phobic core' to all humankind, an inner fear of mortality and of life's fragility that normally, notably in privileged Western cultures, gets packed away into the darkest, most hidden, recesses of the mind. Deep down, everyone knows it. But repeatedly over history, it has been the task of women to create a world which, despite that knowledge, feels safe. Feminicide, then, is the enraged response to women who betray this prescribed essence of the feminine. They are being punished—paying with their lives—for a death that has become too keenly felt. As defences start to crumble, the phobic core of being human explodes. Even as the pandemic seems to diminish in its force, this violence against women has continued, as if the felt fragility of life had released into the atmosphere a new, ugly—and seemingly unstoppable—permission to engage in violence. The numbers of sexual offences are soaring (unlike theft and robbery whose numbers have declined). Domestic violence has become more visible, but the renewed attention has not reduced the prevalence of sexual crime—if anything the opposite.

We are living through an epoch of permanent grief, a time of psychic reckoning that is too much to endure. Cherished illusions are suddenly stripped bare. It is as if the end of illusion, an end that Freud fervently desired in relation to religious belief, had suddenly come upon us without warning, summoning the deepest fears of the soul. It was Freud's argument that religion served above all to keep fear of mortality at bay; his mistake was to think that, for that very reason, any such belief was an illusion that, over time, the powers of the reasoning mind were bound to dissipate (an argument which runs contrary to a basic

tenet of psychoanalysis, that nothing perishes in the unconscious).
Faced with this new psychic dispensation, many rulers across the
globe chose to batten down the hatches, laying down the law as
to what they could, or would not, tolerate, internally and in the
world they claim to own. It does not work. The world refuses
to bend to psychotic conviction, to the omnipotent belief in the
powers of the human mind (Bolsonaro, Trump). In a time of
pandemic it rapidly becomes clear that you cannot force the world
to your will—the wager of dictators throughout history. Nor can
you pretend that the body is within your control. A virus mutates,
shunts invisibly through the atmosphere, carries itself by means
of droplets we cannot even feel on our faces (which is why the re-
assurance provided by wearing masks felt so flimsy). At any given
moment, regardless of the precautions we take, Covid-19 could
be anywhere. At the same time, the unjust, uneven distribution of
vaccinations, which dramatically reduced the number of fatalities
for those privileged enough to receive them, left swathes of people
across the globe still hyper-vulnerable to deadly infection.

Meanwhile, as the quiet backdrop to this story, all women's
hard-won workplace victories in terms of hours, promotions and
equal pay, and in relation to childcare and domestic labour at
home, are in danger of being lost (not that any of this had been
fully achieved pre-pandemic). 'With the schools closed,' Eliot
Weinberger wrote in his essay 'The American Virus,' '45 per cent
of men say they are spending more time home-schooling than
their wives. Three per cent of women say their husbands are
spending more time home-schooling than they themselves are.'
The problem, then, is not only that women were sent back to
the home, where they took on the lion's share of domestic work,

home schooling, and everything else; it is also that, according to a well-worn tradition and grievance, this reality was unseen. (I remember my shock as a young woman when a friend made the obvious point that the success of domestic work is measured by its ability to wipe out every last trace of itself.) Angela Merkel warned of a creeping 'retraditionalization' of roles. The domestic workload of women in France tripled between March and May 2020. In Spain, more than 170,000 people signed a petition protesting against this 'regression'. In the United Kingdom, the 'early years' sector has been pushed to the brink of collapse: in February 2021, a government report predicted that two thirds of preschool nurseries risked closure within a year. According to the British campaign group Pregnant Then Screwed, more than half of pregnant women and mothers expected the pandemic to permanently damage their careers.

All the more reason to note, as I have discussed elsewhere, that, according to a survey of 194 countries conducted by the Centre for Economic Policy Research and the World Economic Forum in 2020, the countries that dealt better with Covid-19, at least at the outset, were all led by women: Germany's Angela Merkel, New Zealand's Jacinda Ardern, Denmark's Mette Frederiksen, Taiwan's Tsai Ing-wen, Finland's Sanna Marin, Barbados's Mia Amor Mottley—a fact that has received little attention.

These women were exerting a different form of politics—no glint of an ego in flight from its own weakness, no false affirmation, no claim to illimitable power. Perhaps for this reason, such leaders did not hesitate to invoke the other histories and forms of violence at play, no less in need of acknowledgement. Might this attentiveness be more likely to come from those who do not shy away from social violence, past, present and future? We might, for example, contrast Johnson's avoidance of the families of the bereaved with Jacinda Ardern's physical embrace of the survivors of the Christchurch mosque massacre in 2019. Ardern's willingness to refuse anti-Islam prejudice by hugging Muslim men and women has for many made her a model of what a world leader should be. Or we might note how Mia Mottley's handling of the pandemic more or less coincided with the transition of Barbados to a republic, a transition which she presided over with a grace that did not compromise the memory of Britain's death-dealing colonial past. Likewise, her careful listing of the nations facing a death sentence in her call for action against climate catastrophe at COP26 in November 2021: '1.5C is what we need to stay alive—two degrees is a death sentence for the people of Antigua and Barbuda, for the people of the Maldives, for the people of Dominica and Fiji, for the people of Kenya and Mozambique—and yes, for the people of Samoa and Barbados. We do not want that dreaded death sentence and we've come here today to say "try harder, try harder."'

'The evolution of civilization,' Freud wrote in *Civilization and its Discontents*, 'is the struggle for life of the human species.' But to struggle for life, you first have to recognize death as its inevitable outcome, which is why Freud could also assert without contradiction that the human organism wants above all to die after its own fashion. To live, you have to allow death into the frame. You have to open the inner world to what is most painful to contemplate. Today, psychoanalysts—faced with the strained intimacy of the

virtual session—are confronting an outpouring of anguish, un-
bidden memories, and traumas never before spoken of, alongside a
struggle to hold on to one of the few spheres in our culture where
the task is to accept the fullest psychic responsibility for oneself
(psychoanalysis as the opposite of housework in how it deals with
the mess that we make). Needless to say, this shared analytic space
could not be further from a threatening home in which your only
options are to smother your thoughts, get the hell out, or hang on
for dear life. It might be too that such a space, which gives room
to pain and its possible transformations, or something close to
it, is a space in which aesthetic work becomes possible, offering
us another form of creative accountability, providing a counter-
vision in an unequal and collapsing world.

I have overstated the division of the sexes—focusing on the
worst-case scenarios as, under the pressure of the pandemic, the
most forbidding versions of sexual difference have been granted
an ugly new freedom to roam. Thankfully, that division is far
more precarious and less sure than, in its worst incarnation, it so
often appears—or violently claims—to be. Nor, crucially, given
the resurgent racism during the pandemic, is gender division the
only fake and overstated division in our culture, which, under-
scored by the pandemic, is tearing people apart, and mowing
them down, on and off the streets. Nonetheless, the harsh fate of
so many women in lockdown, alongside the gift of women leaders who are beating their unique path through disaster, might
have a lesson to teach us. If the hardest task in the struggle for
life is to give death its place at the core of being human, then
perhaps one reason so many women are being punished during
this pandemic is because they are more willing to do so.

LIFE AFTER DEATH

Reconstruction After Covid

AT THE END OF 2021, when there was hope that the pandemic might become a fading memory, I was asked by *The Guardian* to write about the future, about the afterlife of Covid-19. But the future can never be told. This at least was the view of the economist John Maynard Keynes, who was commissioned to run a series to celebrate the paper's first one hundred years in 1921. The future is 'fluctuating, vague and uncertain', he wrote later, at a time when the mass unemployment of the 1930s had upended all confidence, the first stage on a road to international disaster which both could, and could not, be foreseen. 'The senses in which I am using the term [uncertain],' he explained, 'is that in which the prospect of a European war is uncertain, or the price of copper and the rate of interest twenty years hence, or the obsolescence of a new invention, or the position of private wealth-owners in the social system in 1970.

About these matters there is no scientific basis on which to form any calculable probability whatever. We simply do not know.'

This may always be the case, but the pandemic has brought this truth so brutally into our lives that at moments it threatens to crush the best hopes of the heart which always look beyond the present. We are being robbed of the illusion that we can predict what will happen in the space of a second, a minute, an hour or a day. From one moment to the next, the pandemic seems to turn and point its finger at anyone, even at those who believed they were immune. As long as Covid remains a global presence, waves of increasing severity will be possible anywhere and at any moment in time. Across the world, people are desperate to feel they have turned a corner, that an end is in sight, only to be faced with a future that seems to be retreating like a vanishing horizon, a shadow, a blur. Nobody knows, with any degree of confidence, what will happen next. Anyone claiming otherwise is a fraud.

Only so much faith can be placed even in the governments who have shown the surest touch in dealing with the pandemic. Anyone living under regimes whose acts have felt measured and thoughtful will have watched with dismay the death-dealing denials of national leaders from India to Brazil. No nation is exempt, which is just one reason why the monopoly of vaccinations by the privileged nations is so manifestly self-defeating. If the wretched of the earth are not protected, then no one is. An ethical principle—one which in an ideal world should always apply—is pushing to the fore, taking on an unmistakeable if ghostly shape. Nobody can save themselves, certainly not forever, at the cost of anybody else.

In the UK, many legitimately railed against an incompetent government whose repeated refusal to take measures called for by their scientific advisers led to us having one of the highest death tolls of the Western world. They were guilty of negligence, but they have also violated the unspoken contract between government and governed, by leaving the people alone with their fear. Though officially denied, 'herd immunity' seems to have been the policy at the outset of the pandemic and experimented with again, in the UK possibly as late as the summer of 2021. If the idea of herd immunity has been so disturbing, this is not just because it conjures the image of the virus being given free rein and potentially mutating into vaccine-resistant variants, or because of the sinister undercover calculations of the acceptable number of the dead which it entails. Perhaps even more distressingly, the avalanche of deaths that 'herd immunity' appeared so callously to sanction rubs in our faces the reality that death can happen at any time and eventually comes for us all. 'Let the bodies pile high,' words allegedly spoken (though officially denied) by Boris Johnson, proved hard to dispel, leaving any vestiges of safety in shreds. A stalled economy, whose serious consequences must indeed be recognized, was—or so government priorities suggested—more alarming than mass deaths.

Freud once stated that no one believes in their own death. In the unconscious there is a blank space where knowledge of this one sure thing about our futures should be. If the pandemic changed life forever, it might therefore be because that inability to countenance death—which may seem to be the condition of daily sanity—was revealed as the delusion it always is. To be human, in modern Western cultures at least, is to postpone the knowledge of death away for as long as we can. 'There used to be no house, hardly a room, in which someone had not once died,' the Marxist critic Walter Benjamin wrote in his 1936 essay 'The Storyteller'. On the other hand, he argued that in modern life dying had been pushed beyond the perceptual realm of the living, although his diagnosis did not of course include destitute nations, or anticipate the impending war.

In a pandemic, death cannot be exiled to the outskirts of existence. Instead, it becomes an unremitting presence that seems to trail from room to room. One of the as yet unanswered questions of the present moment is how soon hospitals will return once and for all to curing and caring for life rather than preparing for death, so that doctors and nurses will no longer be faced with the inhuman choice between cancer and Covid-19. 'Not today,' one palliative care nurse found herself saying in the midst of the first wave to patients isolated from their loved ones, the terror visible in their eyes, when they asked her if they were going to die. 'Not today'—she did not even pretend to know more.

What on earth, we might then ask, does the future consist of once the awareness of death passes a certain threshold and breaks into our waking dreams? What is the psychic time we are living? How can we prepare—can we prepare?—for what is to come? If the uncertainty strikes at the core of inner life, it also has a political dimension. Every claim for justice relies on belief in a possible future, even when—or rather especially when—we feel the planet might be facing its demise. This is all the more the case as the pandemic allows the bruising fault-lines of racial, sexual and economic inequality in the modern world to press on our sense of reality for everyone, unavoidably, to see.

The misery of impoverished peoples, the surge of violence against black people, women trapped in their homes during lockdown, assaulted and murdered by their partners—all these realities, each as we have seen with its history of racial and sexual violence, are more present to public consciousness, as they move from the sidelines onto the front page. The psychological terrain is starting to shift. Alongside the terror, and at least partly in response, a renewed form of boldness, itself relying on longstanding traditions of protest, has entered the stage, a new claim on the future, we might say. One by one, people in pursuit of collective responsibility have called out the systematic forms of discrimination that are so often passed off as the norm. People will no longer accept denials that the problem exists, as in the UK government-commissioned Sewell report of March 2021 which rejected the fact of institutional racism; or tolerate the most deeply entrenched hatreds, as captured in the famous photograph of a white couple in St. Louis pointing their gun at Black Lives Matter protestors; or leave unchallenged the studied indifference towards injustice that makes people turn aside and casually assume that this is just how the world is and always will be.

Meanwhile, it has become more and more obvious that endless growth and accumulation of wealth involves an exploitation of humans and resources that is destroying the planet. First, in the pandemic, most likely man-made when the virus crossed the barrier between humans and other animals which many scientists believe was caused by interference in the food chain. This in itself is a consequence of large-scale industrial farms and the wildlife trade which are boosting the production of deadly pathogens—the evidence that this increases the risks of future pandemics is now overwhelming. Secondly, in the bodies of migrants mostly in flight from war zones, washed up on the shores of the so-called 'developed' nations. Then, in the droughts, floods, wildfires, superstorms, heatwaves, earthquakes and hurricanes, under pressure of climate disaster, as if life on the planet had already reached the end of days. Another nurse remembers how, as she walked through the Covid-deserted London streets in March and April 2021, it felt as if 'the Apocalypse had hit'. 'We were terrified of this new disease,' states Dr Maheshi Ramasami, senior clinical researcher on the Oxford AstraZeneca team, who recently described their slow realization of what they were facing: 'There was one moment when somebody said to me, "Is this what the end of the world feels like?"'

Everything is telling us that we cannot go on making all the bad decisions that have been made in the name of progress. Being driven—working harder and harder, making more and more money—is not a virtue or some kind of ethical principle to adhere to, but a sure sign of greed, panic and decay. Shooting oneself into outer space, as Richard Branson and Jeff Bezos have raced against each other to do, is a narcissistic sideshow put on by obscenely wealthy men. That they are men is surely key (the last gasp of the phallus and all that). The sky is no limit. They are most likely unaware of how their ambitions echo the strains of an inglorious past. 'Expansion is everything,' wrote Cecil

Rhodes, mining magnate and Prime Minister of the Cape Colony from 1890 to 1896, 'I would annex the planets if I could.'

Rhodes passed laws to drive black people off their land, limiting the areas where they could then settle. The laws he put in place are considered by many historians to have provided a foundation for what later became apartheid. Rhodes' statue at the University of Cape Town was brought down by student protests in one of the most resonant political actions of the times, but the one outside Oriel College in Oxford is still standing. Either way, the organizing principle and fantasy—colonizing the universe to infinity—endures. 'We know there is life on Mars,' the Associate Administrator of Nasa's Science Mission stated in 2015, 'because we sent it there.' The process is known as 'forward contamination'—you destroy at exactly the same moment that you make something grow. In March 2021, one of Musk's space ships crashed back to earth in Texas. 'We've got a lot of land with nobody around, so if it blows up, it's cool,' he is reported to have observed in response to earlier local complaints in Boca Chica village and Brownsville. The crash scattered debris over the fragile ecosystem of state and federally protected lands in the Lower Rio Grande Valley, a national wildlife refuge which is home to vulnerable species.

It is surely no coincidence that such Faustian pacts are being struck at a time when the fragility of life on earth has never been more glaring. These intrepid space explorers remind me of the stinking rich individuals who try to barter with the boatman on their way to the island of the dead in Philip Pullman's *The Amber Spyglass*—the last novel in his trilogy, *His Dark Materials*. Bezos is said to be pouring millions into Alto Labs, a Silicon

Valley gene reprogramming company searching for the secrets of eternal life. They think their money will save them, while the bodies of the less privileged crumble and fail (the sums already spent on these space extravaganzas would pay for vaccines across the world for everyone). This much seems clear. If we want to prepare for a better, fairer, life—if we want to prepare for any kind of future at all—we must slow the pace and change our relationship to time.

So what happens if we enter the realm of psychic time, the inner world of the unconscious where the mind, which we can never fully know or master, constantly flickers back and forth between the different moments of a partly remembered, partly repressed life? This is a vision of human subjectivity that completely scuppers any idea of progress as a forward march through time. The British psychoanalyst D. W. Winnicott, writing in 1949, described a patient who had to go looking for a piece of their past in the future, something they could barely envisage in the present and which, when it first happened, had been too painful for them to fully live or even contemplate. Seen in this light, the relentless drive to push ourselves on and on as if our lives depended on it—killing us more likely—reveals itself as an impossible effort to bypass inner pain. The first hysterical patient in the history of psychoanalysis—analyzed by Freud's colleague Josef Breuer—fell ill as she sat nursing her dying father, overwhelmed by an inadmissible combination of resentment and sorrow. Her anger at the suffocating restrictions of her life was a feeling which, as a young Viennese daughter, she could not allow herself, at least consciously, to entertain. Even without a pandemic, it is rare for such agonizing ambivalence towards those we love and lose to be spoken. There is a limit to how much we can psychically tolerate. This remains the fundamental insight of psychoanalysis, never more needed than today.

When, in April 2021, Boris Johnson slipped under night cover to visit the Covid-19 memorial wall along the Thames, avoiding daytime mourners, an act generally seen as an insult to all those whom the wall is designed to commemorate; or when he blustered and refused for eighteen months to meet the bereaved families of people who had died of the pandemic, he was refusing public accountability, while at the same time making a statement, no doubt unintentionally, about what he could not bear to countenance. He eventually met and assured the families that there would be a public enquiry for which, somewhat unpromisingly, he announced that he would take personal charge himself (he resigned without fulfilling the promise). His behaviour illustrates the gulf between official life and the inward life of the mind. Grief brings time shuddering to a halt. As beautifully rendered by poet Denise Riley after the death of her son, it is time lived without its flow. When you are grieving there is nothing else to do but grieve, as the mind battles against a knowledge which no one ever wishes to own. Even the term 'the bereaved' is misleading as it suggests a group apart and something over and done with, as if you can neatly place to one side and sign off on something which feels, for the one afflicted, like an interminable process (which must feel interminable, at least to begin with, if it is ever to be processed at all).

Seen in this light, Johnson's 'boosterism', his boyish insouciance as it became famously known, appears to be a psychological project. What had to be avoided at all cost was any glimmer of anguish. At the risk—once more—of wild analysis, I would hazard a guess that this began in childhood, as the strategy of the eldest son of a depressed mother for whom he must never stop smiling in order to keep her alive. (Charlotte Johnson Wahl's depression as a young mother is publicly known.) 'I will never forget the pain of the children running down the hospital corridor,' the family nanny stated, 'and having to leave again.' Instead, anything can and must be managed. Everything is going to be all right, a mantra whose irreality has never been more glaring. 'Troubles come and go . . . Disasters are seldom as bad as they seem'—the wisdom of Queen Elizabeth II as described by Johnson in his speech to the House of Commons the day after she died (others might see her ability, in the worst moments, to face the awfulness of the hour as her strength).

According to this ethos, all that matters is the endlessly deferred promise of good times ahead. Hence too, I would suggest, the evasions and obfuscations—from climate change, to 'levelling up', to social care—for none of which has there ever been anything sufficiently ambitious or well-resourced to be dignified with the word 'plan'. The same goes for the fiasco of 'freedom day' on 19 July 2021, when most remaining pandemic restrictions were lifted in the UK, a day people in England were exhorted to celebrate. Marked by soaring cases and chaos over isolation policy, for many in the UK and across a tensely watching world, it felt instead like an occasion for dread. 'Needless suffering', 'disastrous myopia' is how observers from New York to the capitals of Europe described UK government recklessness as cases then steadily rose close to their highest levels. Each time, the same pattern. The political reality of the moment is ignored by subduing the difficult forms of mental life which would be needed in order to face it.

In one of his most famous statements, Freud described the hysterical patient as suffering 'mainly from reminiscences'. From that moment on, psychoanalytic thought has committed itself to understanding how flight from the past traps people in endlessly repeating time, robbing them of any chance for a life that might be lived with a modicum of freedom. You have to look back, however agonizing, however against all your deepest impulses, if you are to have the slightest hope of getting to a new stage. This too has become more obvious as people are crossing over from the space of intimacy and privately stored memories to telling their stories in the public domain. When women step up—and it is mainly if not exclusively women—to recount harrowing tales of sexual abuse from bygone years, it is part of a bid to claim the past as the only way of enabling a future to emerge no longer blocked by violent memory. When a group of British Airways passengers and crew, who had been taken hostage and held as human shields by Saddam Hussein in 1990 at the start of the Gulf War, insisted in summer 2021, after decades of obfuscation and silence, that their story be told, it was their way of saying that the past will never sleep as long as their historic and continuing trauma is unknown (the flight was on a secret UK spy mission authorized by Margaret Thatcher when Hussein's troops were already lined up on the border of Kuwait). 'We can't move on with our lives,' a mother whose child died of haemophilia in the 1980s said last year. The child had been contaminated with HIV from a transfusion of untreated blood—a scandal which the then-Health Secretary, Sir Kenneth Clarke, refuses to own to this day (forty years after the scandal, in August 2022, interim payments were announced for the survivors, but thousands of the parents and children of victims have still received nothing). Each of these hitherto untold stories indicate a new opening. During lockdown, psychoanalysts reported a flood of untold memories from their patients, as if the physical distance and reduced intimacy of the virtual session, combined with the sheer urgency of the moment, were finally giving them the courage to speak.

One glance at today's culture wars will confirm how central this type of reckoning is to our ability to understand the political controversies of the present. What is causing the most trouble, provoking the strongest rebuttals and hatred, is the fearlessness with which the damaged, disadvantaged and dispossessed are calling up the legacy of the past as their passage to a viable future ('manufacturing offences from the past' in the words of Gavin Williamson, the Secretary of State for Education sacked by Johnson in 2021). Their resolve to combat historic and entrenched injustice is surely exemplary. Most vocal of all has been the anger unleashed by the project to bring down the statues of imperial magnates—beginning with Rhodes—or to acknowledge that colonial Britain was involved in the slave trade at all.

At the time of abolition, British slavers were bought off by the government with compensation worth $17bn. Those funds have massively increased over hundreds of years, leaving the next generations to enjoy levels of prosperity that—not surprisingly and even in the face of incontrovertible scholarship and evidence—they have shown themselves reluctant to accept as sourced in such ill-gotten gains. When 'The Legacies of British Slavery', the University College London database charting this history, first opened in 2016, within days it was flooded in almost equal measure by those wishing to know the truth of the past and those wishing no less fervently to deny it.

'My terror of forgetting,' wrote the Jewish scholar Yosef Hayim Yerushalmi, 'is greater than my terror of having too much to remember.' He was writing in the 1980s at a very different moment, when it was a subject of public debate as to whether Klaus Barbie, the Nazi war criminal, should be put on trial. A friend had sent Yerushalmi a poll in *Le Monde* which asked its participants whether the word 'forgetting' or the word 'justice' best summed up their attitude to the events of the war and the occupation of France. Is it possible, Yerushalmi asks, that the opposite of forgetting is not memory, but justice? My answer is 'both'—they are inseparable. There can be no struggle for justice without a vision of the future, so long as we do not lose sight of the worst of the past. We all need to become the historians of our public and private worlds.

One place to begin would be to make room for the complex legacies of the human mind, without the need to push reckoning aside. Past wrongs would not be subject to denial, as if our personal or national identities depended on a pseudo-innocence which absolves us of all crimes. Let the insights of the analytic couch percolate into our public and political lives and, no less crucially, the other way round (we need to acknowledge the weight of historical affliction on our dreams). Social trauma and injustice must not be seen as belonging to another universe from our most wayward fears and desires. Instead they should both find their place at the negotiating table, as we tentatively begin to forge the outlines of a better world. Meanwhile, taking responsibility for failure in relation to the pandemic would help: the cry for redress, for official investigations, or simply for public acknowledgement of the avoidable disaster which millions have been living, from the UK to India to Brazil—although none of this will bring back the thousands who should not have died in the first place.

In psychoanalytic thought, failure and fragility are a crucial part of who we are (only by knowing this can we make the best of our lives). Failure too has a strong political resonance, as many of us anxiously waited to see what might happen in Afghanistan: whether the collapse of the Western powers in a country in which they had been so financially and militarily invested for two decades would be a game-changer; or whether, instead, despite the more or less unanimous agreement that we were witnessing a catastrophic failure of policy, any such recognition would turn out to be a fleeting gesture with nothing learnt, no more than a pause in the preparations for endless war. Squabbling over whether the US is a 'big' or 'super' power—according to Ben Wallace, UK Defence Minister at the time, only a nation willing to exert global force has a right to the second epithet—was hardly reassuring.

So, how then will the pandemic be lived when it is no longer—as we can only hope—at the forefront of people's consciously lived lives? How will it be remembered? Will it be a tale of vaccine triumph, with no mention of the murderous injustice of unequal global distribution; a story of government negligence and accountability; or an acceptance of the ongoing grief for the dead? Responding to a suggestion to make the memorial wall permanent, the artist Rachel Whiteread suggested it should be 'left just to be and then gradually disappear. To have its quietness.' You cannot, she stated, memorialize something that is still going on; a more permanent memorial will need distance and time. When we reach that point, the challenge will be to resist the temptation to brush everything under the carpet, as if the best hope for the future were to go back to normal and blithely continue with matters as they were before: push death aside, treat swathes of the earth's inhabitants as dispensable, drive the planet to its end. On the other hand, a world that makes room for memory *and* justice would be something else. There is still everything to play for.

IN EXTREMIS

*Simone Weil and
the Limits of Justice*

TO BEGIN WITH THE life of the mind, with its capacity for joy, which is not the form of emotional experience most readily associated with the multiple catastrophes—pandemic, war, climate disaster—of the hour. In 1937 and 1938, on the eve of imminent war, Simone Weil made two trips to Italy which, by her own account, were among the happiest experiences of her life. 'For some years,' she wrote to the young medical student Jean Posternak, 'I have held the theory that joy is an indispensable ingredient in human life, for the health of the mind.' Absence of joy, she suggested, is the 'equivalent of madness'. Shortly before her trip, which began in Pallanza on Lake Maggiore, and took in the artistic and religious treasures of Milan, Florence and Rome, she had met Posternak who was a patient in the hospital to which she had been admitted for recurrent and intensifying headaches which plagued her for most of her days.

At times, they were so debilitating that her only wish was to die. 'Joy' is perhaps not the most obvious word to attach to the philosopher Simone Weil. On the other hand, the epithet of 'madness' has constantly trailed her, mostly coming from those, including Charles de Gaulle, who could not fathom her. Perhaps it is Weil's ability to skirt these two extremities of mental and psychic life which allowed her to penetrate so deeply into the social cruelties and injustice of her time and, as I argue, our own.

In fact, it is central to Weil's unique form of genius that she knew how to identify the threat of incipient madness for the citizens of a world turning insane. A straight line runs through her writing from the insufferable cruelty of modern social arrangements—worker misery, swathes of the world colonized and uprooted by 'white races', force as the violent driver of political will—to the innermost tribulations of the human heart. What would it mean, under the threat of victorious fascism, not to feel that you might go crazy?

She was the relentless diagnostician of her era. During the course of her Italian visit, Weil encountered several fascists, including a friend of Posternak who stated, in response to her outspoken anti-fascism, that her 'legitimate and normal' place in society would be down a salt mine (another fascist she challenged in a cinema threatened to have her arrested only to scurry out of the room when their paths crossed again). Weil reacted to the suggestion of the salt mine almost with glee. Surely, she wrote, it would be less suffocating than the political atmosphere above ground: 'the nationalist obsession, the adoration of power in its most brutal form, the collectivity (Plato's "great beast"), the camouflaged deification of death'. Likewise, France on the eve of the Second World War was living in a 'morally unbreathable atmosphere', as it fought against the ignominy of demotion to a second-class power, while still 'intoxicated' by Louis XIV and Napoleon who believed himself to be an object 'both of terror and love to the whole universe'. 'An incredible amount of lying, false information, demagogy, mixed boastfulness and panic' were the consequence of the deluded public mood. She could be describing the UK in the throes of Brexit, or the US, faced with the ascendancy of China, or Vladimir Putin as he wages war in a desperate attempt to restore Russian glory and stave off a similar fate. For Weil, such lament was misplaced. 'Freedom, justice, art, thought and similar kinds of greatness' are not the monopoly of the dominant nations. Far from it. Think small—one of her favourite words was 'infinitesimal'—if you want to create a more equal and peaceable world. 'French sanity,' she concluded her 1938 letter to Posternak, 'is becoming endangered. To say nothing of the rest of Europe.'

Weil is best known as a political philosopher. She was also a revolutionary trade-union activist and a mystic who devoted her last years to the search for sacred truth; a Jew who turned to Catholicism, rejecting her heritage and faith; and also a classicist, a poet, an occasional sculptor, and the author of one unfinished play. 'Why,' she proclaimed in her letter to Posternak, 'have I not the infinite number of existences I need?' She was haunted, she told him, by the idea of a statue of Justice—a naked woman standing, knees bent from fatigue, hands chained behind her back, leaning toward scales holding two equal weights in its unequal arms, so that it inclines to one side. For aesthetic reasons, she had given up on an earlier idea that the figure's feet would also be in chains as this would not be 'so sculptural'. Despite the weight and weariness, the woman's face would be serene. As so often in Weil's writing, it is almost impossible not to read this image as a reference to herself, although her political and moral vision always looked beyond her own earthly sphere of existence, which she held more or less in steady contempt. She may have been sculpting herself in her dreams, but her template was universal. Justice was for all or for none, something to yearn for even if almost impossible to achieve (the feet were unchained, but the statue's hands were tied behind her back).

The fact that Justice was a woman was not incidental. According to Simone Pétrement, Weil's biographer and one of her closest friends, Weil's mother told her that killing to prevent a rape was the one exception she made to the commandment that one should not kill. Much later, Weil would take the image of a young girl refusing—with an 'upsurge' of her whole being—to be forced into prostitution as the model of a true politics. Antigone and Electra were her heroines, both belonging to the Greek lineage in which she sourced the cultural values she most cherished in the modern Western world (she translated central passages from Sophocles' plays). Antigone in particular she returned to at the end of her life, for her appeal to an unwritten law that transcends natural rights which, as she saw it, always sink into the individual claim. The Greeks, she insisted, had no notion of rights: 'They contented themselves with the name of justice.'

Albert Camus was one of the earliest devotees of her writing, although this fact is little known. In a special issue of the *Nouvelle revue française* dedicated to Weil in 1949, he described justice as the principle to which the whole of her work was 'consecrated' (he recognized that this had been her spiritual calling). Justice, then, should 'surely guarantee her a place in the first rank', a prize that she had so 'stubbornly refused' when alive. Yet Weil, he pointed out, had once described conquest as the '*ersatz* of grandeur', and 'sought to conquer nothing'. She was, he wrote to her mother in 1951, 'the sole great thinker of her time'.

Camus did all he could to fulfil his own prediction. He was the editor of the series 'Espoir' at Gallimard which over time would publish seven of her works, tracing the arc of her writing from *La condition ouvrière*, her acclaimed account of the human degradation of factory work, which she experienced at first hand in 1934–1935, to her final extended essay, *The Need for Roots*, a meditation on the evil of displacement, precipitated by her own exile from France during the war. The arc is continuous, the two works connected—in Weil's harrowing account, the worker is an exile, an alien, a human who is uprooted on their own shores. Camus described *The Need for Roots* as 'terrible and pitiless in its audacity', while reaching 'rare heights of thought'.

Weil never stopped writing even though, apart from a scattering of essays, hardly any of her works were published during her lifetime. One exception was 'The *Iliad*, or the Poem of Force', which she herself published in *Cahiers du Sud* in two parts in December 1940 and January 1941. She was convinced that she would be forgotten, a prospect that did not appear to dismay her. In one of her last letters to her parents in July 1943, she wrote of her inner certainty that she contained within her a deposit of pure gold that should be passed on but most likely wouldn't be: 'This does not distress me at all.' Weil herself was a refugee—she described herself as an exile wherever she found herself. Together with her parents, as a young woman of thirty-one, she had fled the imminent Nazi occupation of France to New York, having first travelled to Marseille on the last train to leave Paris on 13 June 1940.

She felt she had deserted her people, and when she arrived in America insisted on going to London, despite her parents' objections, in the sole hope of joining the forces of resistance across the Channel. Her final letters, brimming with optimism, kept her parents completely in the dark about her rapid physical decline. In April 1943, she had been admitted to Middlesex hospital with tuberculosis from which she had no chance of recovering given that she refused to eat any more than the rations of her compatriots in France. 'Hope,' she instructed them in one of her last letters, 'but in moderation.' She was thirty-four years old when she died.

After her death, her parents devoted themselves to the painstaking transcription of her work, including every word of the flood of writing produced during her final months, which is now considered to include some of her most important work. According to her niece Sylvie Weil, born three months before Simone's death, the question of ownership—where the reams of paper should be housed, how they should be published—effectively tore her surviving family to pieces (Sylvie was the daughter of Simone's only brother, the no less distinguished mathematician André Weil). 'You have,' she reproaches Simone in her memoir, 'bequeathed these ruined faces to me.' Lawsuits, and routine 'kidnappings' of the texts by her parents and then her brother each of whom considered themselves to be the legitimate inheritors of her work, saw the material deposited in the Bibliothèque

Nationale, only to be retrieved and then seized again (the parents and André were never reconciled). Meanwhile, according to Sylvie, key figures in the Parisian intellectual world, who she does not name, did all they could to inflame the strife that dominated her childhood until Selma Reinharz, Simone's mother, died in 1965. In the years since her daughter's death, Selma had made what she believed to be her daughter's cause as a writer her own. 'Simone,' Sylvie observes, 'had already been transformed into a saint, and Selma into the saint's mother.'

There is no unifying thread through the writings of Simone Weil, and any attempt to create one risks compartmentalizing her ideas, creating false distinctions and separations. On the page her concepts slide into and out of each other in a sometimes creative, sometimes tortured amalgam, a blur. Weil's writing is like an intricate tapestry with multiple strands—pull on one and it can feel as if the whole thing will fall apart in your hands. Justice, however, stands out. Weil's heart was set on justice. It was her refrain. A recurring principle in pretty much every stage of her writing from start to finish, the concept of justice renders futile any attempt—though many have tried—to separate out Weil the mystic from Weil the activist; or Weil, the lover of God, from Weil the factory worker, who felt that the only way to understand the iniquities of the modern world was to share the brute indignities of manual labour which reduced women and men to cogs in the machines which they slaved for, where every second of labour is measured without mercy by the ticking of a clock. As if, Weil wrote, someone were endlessly whispering in your ear, 'You are nothing,' 'You do not count.' 'You are here to bend, to submit, to shut up.' It was a type of living death which Weil herself barely survived (if war turned man into a thing by killing, factory work turned human beings into a thing while they were still alive). Of course, today, labour is not predominantly factory-based—but as I read her account, images of exhausted workers at Amazon warehouses, and of Indian and Thai sweatshops providing cheap goods for the West, kept appearing before my eyes.

Weil changed her mind a number of times, most significantly when she rejected her earlier pacifism in favour of all-out support for the war against Hitler. She also lost her faith in any version of politics grounded in parties and trade unions, or in what she increasingly came to see, from the Hebrews and Romans to Hitler, as the inevitably totalitarian powers of state; her unqualified inclusion of the Hebrews in that list is seen by many as the most compromised and treacherous component of her writing. But on certain matters she never falters. Right to the end, she grappled with the question of how to conduct oneself in the service of a more equitable world. 'The Christian (by instinct if not by baptism) who, in 1943, died in a London hospital because she would not eat "more than her ration"', wrote former pupil Anne Reynaud-Guérithault in her introduction to Weil's *Lectures in Philosophy*, 'was the same person I had known, sharing her salary in 1933 with the factory-workers of Roanne.'

Measuring her food portions served no one, but in both cases, Weil was weighing her own actions in the scale of justice. Far from being a narcissistic act, as these forays are characterized by her critics (serving her own conscience or slumming it),

Weil's work in factory and farm is better understood as her way
of enacting the proposition advanced in 1971 by the legal theorist John Rawls that justice will only be done when humans are
willing to envisage themselves—or in her case, actually to put
herself—in the place of the disadvantaged and oppressed. 'Only
if you believe your place is on the lowest rung of the ladder,' she
wrote in her Marseille notebook of 1941–1942, 'will you be led
to regard others as your equal rather than giving preference to
yourself.' Joining the anarchists against Franco's forces in Spain
might then be seen as part of the same pattern, likewise her keen-
ness to fight in the Resistance in occupied France, or her pleading with de Gaulle's Free French movement to adopt her plan to
parachute a small group of nurses into France (she took a first
aid course so that she could be one of them). 'What has always
horrified me in war before all else,' she wrote in 1938 to Georges
Bernanos, author of *Les grands cimetières sous la lune* (published
in English as *A Diary of My Times*) which famously exposed the
atrocities committed by the Francoists during the Spanish Civil
War, 'is the situation of those who find themselves at the rear.'

Weil wanted to be in the thick of it. At eleven years old,
living in Paris, she had joined a demonstration of workers demanding shorter hours and higher wages; a year later, she was
back on the streets on behalf of the unemployed. In the 1930s,
while teaching philosophy at the lycée in Le Puy in the Haute-
Loire, she organized and led a demonstration of unemployed
workers who had been given the thankless task of breaking
stones in the city square. She was charged with incitement and
threatened with dismissal from her teaching post. When the
committee asked her to explain why she had been seen in a café

with a worker, she replied, 'I refuse to answer questions about my private life'. *Le Charivari*, a Parisian weekly, described her as 'the Jewess, Mme Weil', a 'militant of Moscow' (the episode came to be known as 'The Simone Weil Affair').

According to other reports, the 'Anti-Christ' had arrived in Le Puy wearing silk stockings and dressed as a man. Only the second was true; Weil wouldn't have been seen dead in silk stockings. She cross-dressed all her life. On one occasion she agreed to accompany her parents to the opera on condition of being allowed to wear a specially made tuxedo. Her mother did her utmost to encourage in her the 'forthrightness' of a boy rather than the 'simpering graces' of a girl. As a young woman, she signed her letters to her mother: 'Your son, Simon.' 'André,' writes Sylvie of her father, Simone's brother, 'never described his sister as a woman . . . He did not talk about her the way one talks about a woman.' Simone only knew her niece, Sylvie Weil, for three months at the very end of her life, but she took the keenest interest in saving her from coquetry: 'I beg you,' she wrote to her parents about their new granddaughter, 'to protect her from exchanging smiles with admirers! I assure you that her personality is already starting to form.'

Weil brooked no compromise. Much later, in a letter from New York in 1942, she explained to an old friend from her school years, Maurice Schumann, that she only sought hardship and danger because the oppression of others pierced her body and soul, 'annihilating' her faculties (Rawls never asked what it might actually feel like to identify with, let alone share the experience of, those at the bottom of the social pile). Action alone would allow her to avoid 'being wasted by sterile chagrin'.

But she was not martyring herself. She was demonstrating, in her person, a form of universal accountability. 'I envied her,' Simone de Beauvoir stated, 'for having a heart that could beat right across the world.' Today we can only be struck by how far her final plan—nurses risking their lives in the service of care—mirrors what we have witnessed in hospitals everywhere in response to Covid-19, a new form of global solidarity which has been one of the few positive outcomes of a pandemic that has also laid bare and exacerbated the world's inequalities. It was this plan, which she held onto passionately till the very end, that led de Gaulle to dismiss Weil as a madwoman. Struck low by repeated rejection, she felt that she risked dying of grief (a good reason not to rush to classify her death as suicide, as many did, including her coroner). According to Simone Pétrement, none of those who were with her in London—with the one exception of Mme Rosin, a German refugee who Weil had known since 1934—believed that she wanted to die.

A central question, one that has vexed much political thought, would then be: Why is justice so elusive? Weil's struggle with this question makes her a psychologist of human power. 'Everyone,' wrote the Athenian historian and army general Thucydides in lines she quoted more than once, 'commands wherever he has the power to do so.' No one can resist mastery over others, because the alternative—to be dominated—is so wretched. 'We know only too well,' the quotation continues, 'that you too, like all the rest, as soon as you reach a certain level of power, will do likewise' (that 'you' is generic and aimed at everyone). Justice therefore requires, before anything else, a laying down of arms, in both senses of the term. It requires a 'supernatural virtue', Weil comments, because, however advantaged you might be, justice requires you to behave as if everyone in the world were equal; 'supernatural' therefore suggests both inspired by divine grace, and requiring super-human effort, as if it were almost too much to ask of anyone.

These reflections on power come right in the midst of her 1942 text *Attente de Dieu*, her deepest meditation on God. 'The true God is God conceived as almighty, but as not commanding everywhere he could.' (This makes God the one exception to Thucydides's rule.) In fact, God only brings 'the universe into existence by consenting not to command it'. Through Creation, God renounced being 'everything'. To revolt against God because of human misery is to represent God 'as sovereign', or as a tyrant, who rules the world, as opposed to a deity who lays down his power. It then falls on humans to create a better world: a form of freedom, or divine abandonment, or both.

Most often translated as *Waiting for God*, *Attente de Dieu* might also be rendered as *God's Expectation*; it is God who is waiting for man to fulfil this promise. To do so, he must relinquish the misguided conviction, cherished by the strong, that the justice of their cause outweighs that of the weak. Nothing, we might say, perpetuates injustice as much as the belief of the privileged that their privilege is just. Or, as Weil observes in her Marseille notebook, 'the rich are invincibly led to believe they are someone'. In an unstable world, Weil observes in one of her finest essays, 'Personhood and the Sacred', written during her last months in London, the privileged seek to allay their bad conscience either by defiance: 'It is perfectly fine that you lack the privileges I possess'; or through bad faith: 'I claim for each and every one of you an equal share in the privileges I myself enjoy.' The second, she comments, is condescending and empty; the first is simply odious. If US conservatism seems unapologetic in affirming the former, British Conservatism has historically oscillated between the two. Today, the idea of 'checking your privilege' has entered the public lexicon, to be met with a barrage of criticism—as if keeping an eye on the advantages you enjoy at the expense of others somehow makes it all OK (hardly what Weil had in mind). She is light-years ahead of her time.

Weil's concept of 'decreation' is undoubtedly her most difficult. In the moment of creation, God shed bits and pieces of himself, which makes human beings the debris of a gesture which leaves neither God nor humans complete. In one of the strongest early commentaries on Weil, Susan Taubes, best known for her 1969 novel *Divorcing*, unravels Weil's proposition that human existence is 'our greatest crime against God'. Man must struggle to detach himself from worldly being in order to restore to God what he has lost. He must also reconcile the idea of affliction as something man-made, and affliction as a product of divine grace and hence the only sure path back to God. Taubes wrote her PhD on Weil but there is a limit to her appreciation. For Taubes, Weil has turned the twentieth-century proclaimed death of God into a theological principle, creating a negative theodicy: 'The dark night of God's absence is itself the soul's contact with God.' Genuine spirituality resides in the wretchedness of mankind. Suffering must be intolerable for the 'cords that attach us to the world to break'. As Taubes sees it, Weil is finally offering as grave an insult to those who suffer as those who suggest they will be rewarded in heaven or that their suffering serves God's final purpose. Weil, she comments wryly, is being 'logical to the bitter end'. Weil herself knew that she had presented the world with a spiritual conundrum which she had failed to solve. 'I feel an ever-increasing sense of devastation,' she wrote to Schumann sometime between her arrival in London in December 1942 and her admission to the Middlesex Hospital in April 1943, 'both in my intellect and in the centre of my heart, at my inability to think with truth at the same time about the affliction of men, the perfection of God and the link between the two.' She was mortified.

In her opera, *Decreation*, Anne Carson gives the kinder, more poetic rendering of Weil's dilemma: 'When I am in any place, I disturb the silence of heaven by the beating of my heart,' words placed in the mouth of Marguerite Porete, the fourteenth century French mystic who was burnt at the stake and who, along with Sappho and Weil, make up her triad of muses. For Carson, Weil is better understood as creating an erotic triangle between God, herself and the whole of creation: 'I am not the maiden who awaits her betrothed but the unwelcome third.' In her New York notebook of 1942, Weil compared God to an importunate woman clinging to her lover and whispering endlessly in his ear: 'I love you. I love you. I love you' (like all mystics, her faith never detracts from the sensuousness of her writing). Weil, Carson writes, is trying to express a 'profoundly tricky spiritual fact, viz that I cannot go towards God in love without bringing myself along'. 'If only,' the Weil voice laments,

'I could see a landscape as it is when I am not there,' a plea with new resonance today as we face the destruction humans have wrought on the planet.

For Carson, all three women 'had the nerve to enter a zone of absolute spiritual daring,' one where the self or ego dissolves. This is just one moment in Weil's thinking which resonates with psychoanalysis, whose birth coincides with her life. She was born at the end of the decade that saw the publication of *The Interpretation of Dreams*, and died four years after Freud. Weil had taught Freud's concepts of repression and the unconscious in her philosophy classes at the girls' lycée in Roanne in 1933–1934. Although in her notebooks she dismissed the inner life as 'temptation', she was an astute reader of his ideas. The 'danger' (her word) of Freud's work resided in the idea that purity and impurity can coexist in the mind: 'thoughts we do not think, wishes we do not wish in our soul' (like 'wooden horses in which there are warriors leading an independent life'). 'Are there really in our souls,' she objected, 'thoughts which escape us?' It would take some time before she herself would embrace such a radical disorientation of the ego as the only viable spiritual and psychic path to take. 'What we believe to be our ego (*moi*),' she wrote in 1942, 'is as fugitive as a wave on the sea.'

None of this detracts from Weil's passionate presence in her own life. 'If we are to perish,' she wrote in her 1934 essay 'Oppression and Liberty', 'let us see to it that we do not perish without having existed.' How, Carson asks, can we square her 'dark ideas' with the 'brilliant self-assertiveness of her writerly project?' 'The answer is we can't.' Carson considers Weil's thinking, writing and being to be the best riposte to her own afflicted

vision. This seems to me to be more consistent with, and certainly fairer to, Weil as I read her, than Taubes' finally uncom-
promising critique. However bleak the terrain, the fight against
tyranny and injustice never ends. In 'This War is a Religious
War', another of her remarkable London papers, she describes
the idolatry that had overtaken Germany as a mirror held up to
the rest of Europe: 'What we see so hideously before us are our
own traits, only enlarged. This thought must not be allowed, far
from it, to reduce by one jot our energy for the struggle.'

For Weil, at the heart of that struggle were the most fundamental and cherished forms of mental freedom, which were
currently under threat: 'It is often said that force is powerless to
overcome thought,' she wrote as early as 1934 before the extent
of the danger was fully clear, 'but for this to be true there must
be thought.' Likewise, her strongest indictment of factory piece-
work stemmed from the way it robbed the worker of any time
or space for thought: the flash of mental insight, of immobility
and equilibrium, which she saw as proper to all human activity
(a form of contemplation she compared to God in the face of
his creation). Instead of a life measured by the ticking clock,
thought should follow the path of the constellations, an infinite
variety which 'excludes all rules and predictions'. Anything
less, she insisted, and life becomes uninhabitable, impossible to
breathe. It was in defence of such freedom that, despite her conversion and expanding devotion to Christianity, she would not
enter the Catholic Church. 'I do not recognize,' she wrote in her
final thoughts on the love of God, 'any right on the part of the

Church to limit the workings of the intellect or the illuminations achieved by love in the realm of thought.' The wellspring of a crushing totalitarianism, she argued, resides in the use of these two little words: '*anathema sit.*' She refused to be baptized.

In her 'Draft for a Statement of Obligations', which appears to have been one of the last texts she wrote, Weil makes even clearer the indissoluble link between love of God and human obligation. A reality beyond and above this world escapes every human faculty except attention and love, but it can only be recognized by those who bear equal respect to all human beings and 'by them alone'. It enjoins on mankind the 'unique and perpetual obligation' to rectify 'all privations of the soul and of the body likely to destroy or mutilate the earthly life of any human being whoever they may be'. This includes any negligence or brutality which reduces a human subject to the cry: 'Why am I being harmed?' for which, almost invariably, there can never be an adequate reply. Failure to take on this obligation—we might call it a duty of care—on the part of any man into whose hands a human has been placed is a criminal activity; any state whose doctrine constitutes a provocation to such failure is subsisting 'in crime'.

This turns love of God into something like a civic task, or at the very least the sole mode of being through which the evils of the world can even begin to be understood let alone redressed. Remember she is now writing in 1942–1943, in the midst of the Second World War. Hitler's Germany is the criminal state she is talking about. But, even though the full extent of the Nazi genocide was not yet known, her failure at this point to name the Jews is, by general consent, unforgiveable. Weil insists she does not qualify as Jewish under Vichy rule; in response to the 'Statut des Juifs', which she derided, she suggested that the best response for Jews would be for them to assimilate or even disappear; in perhaps her worst moment, she implied that the uprooted Jewish people were the origin of uprootedness in the world, which comes perilously close to making them the cause of their own persecution.

Why, Sylvie Weil asks, could her aunt not see how her political fervour echoed the ancient prophets' zeal? Why was she blind to the glaring affinity between her own politically charged generosity and the core Jewish principle, '*Tzedakah*' or charity, 'a form of justice, a way of restoring balance' (*ba'al tzedek* was a master of justice)? Her paternal grandmother, Eugénie Weil, who had lived by that very principle, was a devout Jewess. Sylvie Weil thus corrects the view—more or less the orthodoxy since Simone Pétrement's biography—that Simone was born into a family of purely secular Jews. In fact the hostility of Simone's and André's mother, Salomea Reinharz (Selma), towards her mother-in-law, provided a constant strain in the family filtering down through the generations. As a young woman, Sylvie smuggled herself into the library on her father's membership card to devour Talmud treatises, Ginzberg's legends and Graetz's history of the Jews. 'You are doing what my sister would have done,' André responds when he finds out, 'because she was honest, by and large.'

Despite this dark shadow, Weil's spiritual journey was far from being an exit from political life and thought. In the words of Gillian Rose, the two were irrevocably 'entwined'. Her encounters with God—in her correspondence and notebooks she talks of three visitations—intensify her earthly commitments, for all the ruthlessness with which she detaches them from the history of her own Jewish antecedents (as regards this part of her legacy, we could say that Simone Weil forgot herself). If there was a turning point in her thinking, it was her experience at the front during the Spanish Civil War, too often dismissed as a bit of a joke because she had to be rescued by her parents when she tripped and immersed her leg in a drum of burning oil, or because, to her credit as I see it, she was useless in aiming a gun. In fact she had every intention of returning as soon as her wound had healed, on condition that her solidarity would not require her to be complicit with spilt blood.

I read this moment as initiating a new level of political understanding which once again strongly resonates with the present. What forms of 'harsh madness', she had asked in her essay on the *Iliad*, does war make human beings capable of? She had already learned from Georges Bernanos and others of the atrocities being carried out by Franco's veterans on the insurgents. Weil went one step further by recognizing those carried out by the insurgents themselves. This included the retaliatory murder of children, the killing of a fifteen-year-old boy who had been offered the choice between death and joining the anti-fascists, which he refused to do, the young baker murdered in front of his father who promptly went mad. All of which led her to recognize fully for the first time the potential for violence, regardless of political affiliation, in everyone: 'As soon as any category of humans is placed outside the pale of those whose life has value, nothing is more natural than to kill them.'

For Camus, this moment inflicted on Weil a 'serious wound' that never ceased to bleed. What repelled her was the hypnotic power of violence, the cunning smiles with which such acts were embraced. Perhaps most shocking of all, as she wrote to Bernanos, were the two anarchists who boasted to her of murdering a couple of priests, only to be 'astonished I didn't laugh'. She had watched peaceable Frenchmen, to whom it would never before have occurred to kill, taking visible pleasure in the bloody atmosphere. Dread that they would appear as lacking in virility is, she suggests, also key. 'Not once have I seen anyone,' she wrote, 'even in complete privacy, express revulsion, disgust or as much as disapproval in the face of pointlessly shed blood.' 'You are,' she wrote to Bernanos, 'the only person, to my knowledge, who has bathed [sic] in the atmosphere of war and resisted.' 'The desire to humiliate the enemy,' she wrote to him, which was 'spilling out' everywhere, 'is curing me once and for all of patriotism.' Up to this point, she had been patriotic with all the 'exaltation of a kid caught up in a war'.

Out of this moment emerges what will become a lifelong commitment to confronting human violence in order not to fall prey to it; a pledge to face up to the darkest night of the soul, to what people and nations, given half a chance, are capable of. There is an analogy, Weil insisted, between what Germany did to Europe and France exacted on its colonies, which would make victory hollow unless it were to be followed by decolonization—to use today's term. 'I must confess,' she had written to Gaston Bergery, editor of the Communist Party newspaper, *La Flèche*, in 1938 when she was still opposed to war against Hitler, 'that to my way of feeling, there would be less shame for France

even to lose part of its independence than to continue trampling the Arabs, Indochinese and others underfoot.' France,
like every other nation, had been only intent on 'carving out
for herself her share of black or yellow human flesh'. 'I cannot
complain,' she wrote to Huguette Bauer from occupied France
in 1940, 'that we are suffering the fate that we have inflicted on
others.' In her 1938 essay on the colonial problem in the French
army, she suggested that it would not be hard to find a colony
ruled by a democratic nation imposing harsher constraints than
those exerted by the worst totalitarian state in Europe. This, as
she knew, was a scandalous observation when democracy was
generally accepted as the only true stake of the approaching
war. But she was right that a democracy made up of opposing
parties had been powerless to prevent the formation of a party
whose aim was the overthrow of democracy itself (something
we are also witnessing today from the 2016 election of Trump
to Orbán in Hungary, Erdoğan in Turkey, Modi in India and
more).

For Weil, colonialism was the exertion of force in its purest
form, uprooting or eradicating the traditions it meets in its path,
destroying all traces of indigenous histories, wiping out the
communities' own memories and then, as the final insult, de-
nying the violence it has wrought ('Simone Weil anti-colonialist'
is the title given by her editors to this section of her collected
works). What follows, in the colonizing nations, is a regime of
'ignorance and forgetting', a whitewash of their own past—her
analysis uncannily predicts today's culture wars, in which the
memory of slave-dealing, or rather the denial of its memory, has
been central. Even the workers involved in the great uprising of

1936, she observed, seemed to have forgotten the existence of the colonies (on questions of race, there can be no guarantee that the stance of the working class will be progressive). Likewise, the revelation of the 1931 atrocities in Indochina barely registered among the 'cultivated' who are meant to be well-informed. The problem, Weil concludes, 'is that, as a general rule, a people's generosity rarely extends to making the effort to uncover the injustices committed in their name'.

Weil is treading on dangerous ground, and not just because of the analogy she makes between Nazism and colonization (when Cameroon philosopher Achille Mbembe made a similar link in a 2021 lecture, he was met with outrage). She is describing what psychoanalysis will subsequently theorize as the process of projection, a way of ridding oneself of anguish which makes it more or less impossible for human subjects, regardless of what they may have done or what might have been enacted in their name, to shoulder the burden of guilt, whether historic or personal. These lines read almost as if they were lifted from the famous Austrian-British psychoanalyst Melanie Klein:

> In so far as we register the evil and ugliness within us, it horrifies us and we reject it like vomit. Through the operation of transference, we transport this discomfort into the things that surround us. But these same things, which turn ugly and sullied in turn, send back to us, increased, the ill we have lodged inside them. In this process of exchange, the evil within us expands and we start to feel that the very milieu in which we are living is a prison.

Weil knew the process of projection first hand. Her headaches made her feel she wanted to besmirch the whole universe with her misery in order not to have to feel, or contain, the pain within her. She also found herself wanting to hit other people on the head (like all acts of projection or acting out, this would have made matters worse). Christianity would then be the reverse of projection, as Christ takes the burden of the world's misery on himself.

In a strange and most likely unintended echo of Freud on the death drive, Weil argues that death is the 'norm and aim of life'. Only if one recognizes 'with all one's soul' the frailty of human life and the mortality of the flesh, and admits that we are a 'mere fragment of living matter', will we stop killing. In her essay on the *Iliad*, she evokes the 'illusion, exaltation and fanaticism' by means of which those who give the impression of having risen to a higher plane 'conceal the harshness of destiny from their own eyes'. She was referring to Greek tragedy and to the Gospels, but the lesson still holds. It is their refusal to acknowledge the reality of death that drives tyrants to seek to subdue their people and colonize the earth. It is the denial of the harshness of human destiny that leads rulers to boast at a time of pandemic—in complete disregard of the measures needed, or of the international spread of the virus, or of the ultimate uselessness of any non-global vaccination policy—that they have the situation completely under control. They need do nothing, whatever fatalities, in the UK and Brazil for example, which— like night and day—will then surely follow.

Weil is precise in her historical judgements however far they might reach. Here she allows herself a glimmer of hope. Unlike the Roman Empire whose spirit he inherited, Hitler, she predicted in 'The Origins of Hitlerism', would most likely fail to rule the world because he made it his priority to establish a dictatorship at home above all else. The will of a totalitarian state to crush its own subjects overrides and finally defeats its lust for conquest.

The implications of Weil's analyses are, therefore, as political as they are personal and intimate, not least for nations on the cusp of victory. 'The victory of those defending by means of arms a just cause, is not necessarily,' she wrote in the same essay, 'a just victory'. She was pleading with the Allies, when the moment arrived, not to disarm Germany by force. The only way to avoid doing so would be for the victors—'allowing that this is our destiny'—to 'accept for themselves the transformation they would have imposed on the vanquished' (not, we might say, the customary path taken by nations that win wars). Weil is proposing a radical crossing of enemy lines: 'the purest triumph of love, the crowning grace of war', she wrote elsewhere, 'is the friendship that floods the heart of mortal enemies'. Again in anticipation of the challenges of today's world, Weil calls for people from different stations in life, different nations, to acknowledge, against all impulse, that they are all part of the same species. But to make such a move would require each of us to be willing to see ourselves in the least likely or hoped for place. This is a version of Rawls once more, but now with a psychic gloss and an international, military, colonial frame. Against race, class and national affiliations, Weil's heart is beating right across the globe. Why has this psychodynamic aspect of her work received so little attention?

In these moments, Weil outlines a new ethic, one which could be described as a form of magical thinking because, by giving over one's very being to the wretched of the earth ('pauper, refugee, black, the sick, the re-offender'), you are upending the natural revulsion which humans feel towards misery—natural, that is, for those who have even minimally been spared. You are turning disgust into a willing and tender embrace. 'It is as easy,' she suggested, 'to direct the mind willingly towards affliction as it is for a dog, with no prior training, to walk straight into a fire and allow itself to be burnt to death.' An 'upsurge' of energy 'transports' you into the other. You lose yourself in allowing the other to be (contrary to power which expands to fill all the available space). In the final analysis, with the odds piled against it, only such a move makes it possible to recognize the fundamental equality and identity of all people, which means it is also the only chance for justice. It is, then, all the more ironic, that the one leap of identification she herself seemed incapable of making, the one form of historic empathy she refused, was with herself as a Jew.

Weil was going against the grain of what she believed, at the deepest level, humankind to be. She was also going against the grain of her own experience, her feeling of eternal exile, of being radically unloved and incapable of loving herself. In May 1942, she wrote a long letter to the radical Dominican priest Father Perrin. It was her 'spiritual autobiography,' written from the Aïn-Sebaa refugee camp in Casablanca, where she was waiting for

her transit to New York. It was an outpouring. Whenever anyone speaks to her without brutality, she explained, she thinks
there must be some mistake. He was the first person in her life
who she felt had not humiliated her. 'You do not have the same
reasons as I have,' she wrote, 'to feel hatred and revulsion towards
me.' 'It is not by chance,' she had written to herself in one of her
first notebooks, 'that you have never been loved.' In the eyes of
others, she wrote to Perrin, she was 'the colour of a dead leaf, like
certain insects'.

Weil's inspiration is sourced in revulsion, regardless of the
love of those who surrounded her, perhaps above all that of her
mother, whose love Selma herself acknowledged had been too
much for her daughter to bear. But, if Weil repudiated, and felt
herself repudiated by, love, such failing was also to be blessed
with insight and generosity. The risk of loving, she once warned
a former student from Le Puy, was not just that of blindly pledg-
ing one's own existence, but even more, the risk of becoming the
arbiter of another's (the student had written to tell her that she
had radicalized the whole class, turning them all into a bunch
of progressive 'malcontents'). Such revealing moments are often read as indicating a level of despair or mental torment that
disfigures her judgement. Instead, I would argue that it was her
abjection, and above all her willingness to know and to own it,
that propelled her to the heights of her ambition for spiritual
grace, mental freedom and a fairer world. I, for one, can only
marvel at the hill she had to climb.

A final clue as to how she managed her own affliction is to
be found in Weil's way with words. I always come away from
her work with a sense of her dexterity or even playfulness, as

if writing were the one place where she could be most at ease
and loving towards herself. By her own account, she is a creature of analogy, starting with perhaps the most vexed of them
all—between Hitler and ancient Jerusalem, or Nazism and
colonialism. Analogies are deceptive (*trompeuses*), she wrote in
1939, but they are her 'sole guide'. Once you start looking for
them, they are everywhere—remember dogs walking into fires,
unconscious thoughts like warriors concealed in wooden horses,
and God as a clinging woman lover. Elsewhere, a dog barking
beside the prostrate body of his master lying dead in the snow
conveys how futile calling out dishonesty and injustice can feel.
Skin peeled from a burning object it has stuck to evokes the
Frenchman forced to tear his soul from his country after the
1940 fall of France. Or freedom of thought with no real thinking is compared to 'a child without meat asking for salt'. True
labour, whose dignity has been restored—hard to conjure under
capitalist exploitation—is like 'the child about to be born in the
making of the layette'. Nothing exists, Weil states, without its
analogy in numbers (her link to her brother was profound).

  Visceral and unworldly, Weil's analogies push at the limits
of language, giving voice to something painful or that eludes
understanding. God loves, not as I love, but as an emerald '*is*'
green. The fools in Shakespeare (notably in *King Lear*), she writes
to her parents in one of her last letters, 'are the only characters to
speak the truth': 'Can't you see the affinity, the essential analogy between these fools and me?' Analogy is a spiritual principle, since it is only by means of 'analogy and transference'
that our attachment to particular human beings can be raised
to the level of universal love. Weil has often been criticized for

the unyielding tenacity of her judgements but this wrongly tips the scales, ignoring the risks that she takes. At her best, Weil contains multitudes; it is a miracle, she insists, that thoughts are expressible given the myriad combinations which they make. She has the gift of being more than one person and of occupying more than one mental place at a time. In the end, spiritual, ethical and political generosity require you to reach, without limits, beyond yourself. I can think of no other writer in the Western canon who pushes us so far off the edge of the world, while keeping us so firmly, and resolutely, attached to the ground beneath our feet.

AFTERWORD: ON VIRTUE

ON THE OPENING PAGE of his famous 1981 meditation, *After Virtue*, the philosopher Alasdair MacIntyre asks his readers to imagine themselves living in the aftermath of catastrophe. A series of environmental disasters, blamed by the public on the scientists, leads to widespread riots, with laboratories destroyed, instruments wrecked. The government that takes power abolishes science in schools and universities, and imprisons or executes any scientists who remain. By the time they realize their mistake, it is too late. All that is left of scientific knowledge are fragments. MacIntyre's startling hypothesis is that the language of morality has entered 'the same state of grave disorder as the language of natural science in the imaginary world I have just described.' We are living in a world 'after virtue', where any clear moral compass has been lost.

When *After Virtue* was first published, the human destruction of the earth was already advanced. But MacIntyre could not have anticipated how strongly his image of natural catastrophe would resonate. Today it is clear that the march of so-called progress has been tearing the world we live in to shreds, that the good of human individuals, in Western terms at least, and the good of the planet are not—most likely never were—the same thing. How do you take your moral bearings in a world that has gone so awry? In this book, I have concentrated on the cruelty of social arrangements: the fatally uneven response to Covid-19 by governments across the world, the resurgent and abiding inhumanity of war, the torture for many women of 'normal' domestic life. But I have also been in search of slivers of justice, flashes of radical empathy, moments of resistance and solidarity whose urgency becomes all the more pressing as the grounds on which each one relies—whether in terms of individual conduct or broader human understanding—seem, under pressure of global ruthlessness, to be crumbling beneath our feet. For all the inspirational acts of kindness which we have witnessed during Covid-19, we are living at a time marked by the deepest failure of many citizens of the world, and of most nations, in their regard for each other. A time when laying claim to virtue has the death-dealing ring of denial and deceit. Thus Putin claims to be 'purifying', that is, 'denazifying', Ukraine (aggression clothed in noble intent); while UK Home Secretary Suella Braverman announces her latest plan to indefinitely detain migrants who enter the country 'illegally' and bar them from ever settling in the UK (vicious cruelty on behalf of the 'good' of the nation).

MacIntyre's dystopian 'parable' also finds another echo for

today. It is because rage is aimed at the wrong target—scientists held responsible for disaster, like the Chinese laboratories charged with having solely created and unleashed Covid-19—that we find ourselves in such a sorry state. One of the most striking features of the present must surely be the ease with which so many refuse to take responsibility for what has gone wrong, offloading it onto anyone other than themselves. Not to speak of the unequal distribution of pain which, while always true, has been one of the standout features of these past years: the greater death toll of the poor and the racially underprivileged in the face of Covid-19, how the brunt of global warming, precipitated by the economies of developed nations, has fallen most heavily on the inhabitants of the global south. Today, the CO_2 emissions of the global super-rich (125 billionaires to be precise) are equivalent to the output of the whole of France (with a population of 67.5 million). In November 2022, it emerged that the richest nations, notably the US, UK, Canada and Australia, are failing to pay their 'fair share' of a pledged $100bn climate fund to aid developing countries. The same nations which, without the faintest pang of conscience, claim to be doing most to save the planet. 'We were the ones whose blood, sweat and tears financed the industrial revolution,' stated Mia Mottley, Prime Minister of Barbados who, as we have already seen in this book, can be relied on not to mince her words, 'Are we now to face double jeopardy?' According to the UN Secretary General, António Guterres, on the eve of COP27 in November 2021, only a surge in adaptation investment, ensuring additional payments to the most afflicted, poorest nations, will save millions of lives from 'climate carnage'.

In this morass, we might do worse than to take MacIntyre's apocalyptic vision, however counterintuitively, as a guide. Only by recognizing the frailty of our morality, the unsteady hold we have on virtue, or even our perverse capacity, our readiness to embrace the worst on offer, is there the faintest chance of moving to a better place. Nothing is more dangerous than confronting a world full of fear, arms akimbo, with a boast. Or, hanging on in the face of disaster to the idea that we each, individually, are good, that our perfection, lamentably unmatched by an imperfect reality, is something into which the ills of the time—pandemic, climate catastrophe and war—unfairly encroach. According to such a mindset, the more insecure things appear, the more confident, assertive, and controlling we need to become in order to master both the world and ourselves. There is only one step from here to what Simone Weil would call the exertion of force, a form of power whose sole function is to impose itself. Not once does she waver in her conviction that force in this sense, not least the belief in immutable strength which upholds it, will always be found at the opposite moral pole to justice. Being convinced we have moral ownership of the earth is the best way to make it uninhabitable. Perhaps the governments of the Western world are useless on climate because the very thought of catastrophe is so at odds with the idea of earthly power.

We have witnessed the lengths to which politicians will go to keep inequality firmly in place. The lies they tell, the hatred they spawn, the consummate skill with which they take advantage of fear and send it skuttling into the wrong place. I am not just referring to 'fake news', a phrase which risks leaving the categories of truth and falsehood, good and evil in their allotted, norma-tively sanctioned, position. What I am talking about is more visceral. One unregulated digital ad in the November 2022 US mid-term elections used a horror movie soundtrack punctuated by gunfire while a voice-over announced that John Fetterman, a Democratic candidate for a Senate Seat in Philadelphia, had a 'love affair with criminals'. If elected, he would 'keep the drugs flowing, the killers killing and the children dying'. No source for the ad was given beyond the logo 'Citizens for Sanity' which appeared in small type at the end of the video. 'Sanity' is how-ever the give-away. Defying predictions, Fetterman won the seat, but the intention was clear: to provoke a shudder of revul-sion—a 'feel-good' factor of sorts—while convincing voters that the world, or at least the nation, is in serious danger of losing its mental grip (the reference to dying surely also included an allusion to his stroke two days before the State primary in May 2022, feeding on the generalized, Covid-19-intensified, fear of death).

When I was in New York in October, a special issue of the *New York Times* opinion section was devoted to the question of mental health. Among other things it pointed out that 'mental health', with its implication of wellbeing, is slowly being used to refer to its opposite, as in 'X has mental health issues', that is, to those who suffer mentally (healthy is what they are *not*). This blurring of the lines goes hand in hand with a steadfast reluctance to address the myriad social and economic causes of mental breakdown, to acknowledge that such pain is most often the consequence of human decisions: how advantage is distrib-uted, who gains and who loses, how the world is run. At the same time, actions fuelled by far-right incitement are dismissed as one-off mental disturbance, the work of a deranged individual which leaves untouched the broader insanity of political life. 'Let there be no talk of "mental illness",' wrote journalist Jeff Sharlet, cited in one of the essays, with reference to Payton Gendron, an alleged white supremacist charged with the killing of ten black people in Buffalo in May 2022. Gendron's manifesto, he insisted, is 'very cogent, articulate fascist hate', of the kind that has played such a key role in the dramatic escalation of violence against Latinos and Black people over these past years. This is not to say that an individual in distress might not find themselves acting out social hatreds on behalf of everyone else (like the hysteric who, in the psychoanalytic account, brings the unspoken trouble of family life to the surface). Nor that social factors are the sole determinants of psychic anguish. Mostly, however, the idea of one-off mental disturbance is mobilized against political insight. Instead of seeing the injustice all around, we take strange comfort from living in fear of 'freaks'.

We need to watch carefully the way mental distress feeds, and is sucked into, the wider political atmosphere. For Andy Milburn, retired US Marine Colonel, now serving in Ukraine, such distress has been the legacy of his country's military blunders in Iraq, Afghanistan and before that, the disaster of Somalia, from which he returned traumatized. Everything he had ever learned—'all the social trappings of civilized society'—had capsized. He was appalled at how 'shockingly easy' killing could be. Ukraine, on the other hand, was morally clear: 'How many wars are morally unambiguous?' This intervention offered him redemption from his own and his country's past violence, assuaged his guilt, suggesting that one of the purposes served by US intervention in this war is to make good one of the darkest chapters in its own history (one story of killing redeemed by the next).

The US is not alone in turning Ukraine to its own purpose which, in popular rhetoric, becomes at once a beacon of military virtue and the source of all ill. In the UK, Kwasi Kwarteng, briefly chancellor under the doomed premiership of Liz Truss from September to October 2022, blamed the economic crisis on the pandemic and the Russian invasion which, in a striking formula, he described as 'an exogamous, extreme event'. He was implying that the collapse of the UK economy, under pressure of inflation, and the hole about to be blown in the public finances by his own proposed tax cuts and limitless public debt, were the result of forces that had dropped from the skies (as if, indeed, it was the UK rather than Ukraine which had been the object of assault). 'Exogamous' is telling. It suggests that, instead of being the full agents of the political choices we make, we are being forced to marry out of the tribe.

Today, in the field of gender, also central to this book, virtue is being weaponized. The so-called 'ideal' rape victim is a woman to whom her rapist is unknown, who goes straight to the police, or who never returns to an abusive partner, and, most illogical and dangerous of all, must show signs of a violent struggle. Whereas, had she been foolish enough to put up a fight, it would most likely have left her dead. Made answerable for the crime committed against her, she is required to be the embodiment of virtue. Only a ghostly and asexual victimhood, or chastity as it used to be called, will save her.

What happens, then, if we look to the places where moral failing and imperfection are not swept aside, but taken as the foundation, however unsteady, for another, more accountable, way of thought and of life? Even in the realm of Aristotelian virtue, to which MacIntyre makes his appeal against the chaos of the day, there is no guaranteed relationship between what passes for a virtuous action and its outcomes. Courage can sustain injustice (killing as the sign of the brave); loyalty has been known to strengthen murderous aggression (fealty to fascism, or 'defending' one's country by pushing migrants in flight from persecution and war back across the border into harm's way); generosity can weaken the capacity to do good (small or even lavish acts of charity which assuage the conscience while leaving more or less untouched the obscene Covid-induced profits of the super-rich). Likewise taking her cue from the Greeks, Weil makes the link to today. Agamemnon, who sacrificed his daughter, Iphigenia, to release the winds of war, 'lives again in the capitalists who, to maintain their privileges, acquiesce lightheartedly in the wars that may rob them of their sons'. Killing one's children is generally seen as the most evil of all human crimes (*Medea* is the figure who most readily comes to mind). In fact, killing one's sons is hardwired into the human proclivity for war. Capitalism is murderous. Never more visibly than today, when endless growth—the driver and lodestar of the whole system—is systematically destroying the planet.

Virtue, we might say, is a knife that cuts both ways, as Freud famously described the unconscious. He was warning against the risks of invoking the hidden depths of psychic life in the courtroom, as if an imperfect inner life—which must mean any inner life at all—could be summoned in law in order to establish a propensity to crime. For the same reason he insisted that it was not the task of analysis to pass moral judgement on the nature of human drives which in themselves 'were neither good nor bad'. Even in the Second World War, where the moral distribution of vice and virtue are mostly seen as crystal clear, the waters are muddied. Weil was a pacifist until Hitler invaded Poland. She refused to grant her country the moral high ground as long as France retained its colonies, for both of which positions she was branded a traitor. She was also accused of collaborating with Vichy. No one, she insisted, had the right to sit in judgement on Pétain since everyone, herself included, had welcomed the armistice. 'The word traitor,' she wrote to Jean Wahl from New York where she was living in exile in 1942, 'should only be used about those of whom one feels certain that they desire Germany's victory and are doing what they can to this end.' Likewise Freud described psychology as indifferent regarding who committed the crime, its sole concern being to know 'who desired it emotionally and who welcomed it when it was done'. For the rest, Weil continued, some may have 'honourable' motives 'that are justified by particular situations' which we will never know. Others may be constrained by pressures no one could resist unless they were 'heroes'. Most of those who judge have never been tested or tried.

Weil was neither indicting nor exempting herself, but rather occupying a middle ground where people, for whatever reasons, good or bad, equivocate. Those who accuse her of siding with Pétain have therefore missed the point. Her support for the war then became unyielding—she would go on to be part of the Resistance. But she laid claim to neither heroism nor innocence. In fact, she believed herself to be worthless, spending much of her life, in the words of Italian philosopher Roberto Esposito, in 'an uninterrupted battle directed mainly against herself'. In Esposito's reading, Weil read history from its dark side, in search of the 'torn heart' beating from within 'extreme discord', a beat in which she never lost faith. Amidst such discord, the strongest hope would be 'to kill as little as possible', although Weil knew that the very fact of bearing arms wipes out all restraint. Violence always 'obliterates anybody who feels its touch', meaning victim and aggressor alike.

For that very reason, the ability to recognize your own face in the enemy was, for Weil, the purest 'triumph of love', the 'crowning grace', like the mutual admiration of mortal enemies Priam and Achilles in Homer's *Iliad*. What the poet of the *Iliad* sees, and his characters do not, is that the fact of death equalizes everyone in war, as in life. Winning is never just winning, since, by the mere fact of being mortal, everyone is heading for defeat. It was, therefore, a central component of Aristotelian virtue to give death and human vulnerability their due. Exactly what, as we have seen throughout this book, our most fanatical leaders and billionaire entrepreneurs have shown themselves incapable of, as they pour millions into the search for life's elixir and propel themselves into space. Those dying in their thousands during

Covid are then left with sheer meaninglessness, robbed of any moral frame through which they can die their own death. As we have seen, faced with the death of his own daughter from the Spanish flu, Freud came to see this as the aim of all human and organic life. Death has been dehumanized. Near the end of his life, psychoanalyst D. W. Winnicott wrote in his unfinished autobiography, 'May I be alive when I die.'

'I do not know,' writes moral philosopher Judith Shklar, 'why a curious division of labour prevails, why philosophy ignores iniquity, while history and fiction deal with little else.' Alberto Moravia's most famous novel, *Two Women*, published in 1957, also set during the Second World War, is a tale of iniquity in which no one is spared, told from the point of view of two women, a mother and daughter. I alighted on it by chance in the scorching days of summer 2022 at an open air book stall on London's South Bank which has been there since I can remember. I once picked up from the same stall a copy of Rebecca West on Saint Augustine, and the conservatism and political ruthlessness which was the other side of sainthood, at the time no less germane to what I was trying to think about. Moravia's novel turns on the question of what happens to women, as guardians of virtue, when history tears up the rule book. To begin with at least, the mother, Cesira, believes her daughter, Rosetta, to be a saint. Convinced that they will soon be returning to their home on the outskirts of Rome when the US army arrives to liberate them from fascism, they escape to the countryside, bathed in the glow of Rosetta's goodness and their own hopes. They are trying to join Cesira's parents who live in the mountains. What they find is squalor, abandoned and bombed-out villages, putrefying land underfoot, crime and wanton death.

It is not often that a story of war, whether as fiction or nonfiction, is told through the eyes of women—Svetlana Alexievich's first book, *The Unwomanly Face of War*, which relies solely on the oral testimony of Russian women from the Second World War, was hailed on publication in 1985 as an exception. And it's even less common to include the rape of a daughter as witnessed by her mother, and then to track its devastating effects. Rosetta is brutally assaulted inside a disused church, while her mother, fending off her own attackers, somehow manages to escape. Confounding every cliché, Rosetta is sexualized by her experience: 'Something unknown to her had entered her flesh like fire.' Her saintliness is no match for her assailants who turn her from the 'perfect' into the 'imperfect' victim of rape. In search of pleasure, she barters herself to a run of local desperados, evacuees, one of whom she comes to love, and who abandons her, a loss to which she reacts without lament. When Cesira realizes what is happening, she attacks Rosetta, seizes her, bangs her down on her mattress and showers her with blows, while screaming, 'I'm going to kill you.'

In the mind of her mother, Rosetta has turned from saint to a common 'whore'; but the hardest reckoning takes place between Cesira and herself, as she discovers that she is capable of uncontrollable violence towards the person she loves most in the whole world. Something unknown has also entered her flesh like fire, in her case the desire to kill (which means in fact that neither the mother nor the daughter escaped). She had already understood that such violence is not alien to human conduct but is simply unleashed by the permissions of war. It is something that erupts when laws, respect for others, and fear of God have been suspended, and men act without restraint. To that extent, war changes nothing: 'You were simply waiting for a war, the whole lot of you,' she shouts at a bunch of crooks who harboured and then cheated the two women near the end of the book, 'so that you could let yourselves go and do all the things that you would never have dared to do in normal times.'

Cesira is the moral barometer for a world whose measure cannot be taken. Waking from a dream in which Nazis and Fascists were being shot, she is appalled to find herself enjoying 'the destruction of other people with the same feeling with which one enjoys the coming of spring and the flowers and the weather.' How can it be, she asks, that a ferocious Nazi, a man they encounter by chance in the mountains, who found special enjoyment in burning people alive with a flamethrower, could also show himself to be attuned to injustice (he challenges a lawyer who has taken flight from the plains to justify the ample provisions of his table when peasants are dying of hunger)? How could Rosetta turn so resolutely from virtue to vice, throwing herself into each with equal, perfectly devoted, commitment?

The hardest lesson to be learned is the danger of ever believing in purity or perfection—your own or your daughter's, or that of anyone else—however closely you might hold them within your most fiercely guarded and intimate inner space. The idea of perfection is a decoy. It is not a thing which you receive at birth or a gift of nature; or if you do, it is only ever on loan and sooner or later you will lose it, 'all the more disastrously for having been confident of possessing it'. Cesira explains the moral of her own story:

> In short, it is almost better to have been born imperfect and gradually to become, if not perfect, at any rate better, than to be born perfect and then be forced to abandon that first transient perfection for the imperfection that life and experience bring with them.

Better to start with imperfection, which leaves room for growth, than with stultifying virtue from which there is no clean exit (a point which, once again, feminism has been making for centuries). After all, even the Aristotelian virtues were not attributes to be hoarded, but qualities to strive for in pursuit of a fulfilled and fair life. The delusion is to believe that moral purity and perfection are possessions, that imperfection is shameful, that violence is a spanner in the works, rather than part of the inner portion of everyone. By itself, awareness of this will not be enough to save us. But making space for such precisely imperfect knowledge within the scope of human understanding will surely slow things down. It might just help prevent the spread of devastation as it travels with such indecent haste across our futures.

London, 6 December 2022

NOTES

5 *'centuries old and unchanging'*: Neil Macfarquhar, 'What Russians see in the news', *The New York Times*, 23 August 2022.

5 *'lives by the holy conviction that it will exist for ever'*: Oleksandr Mykhed, 'We will rebuild everything', *Financial Times*, 31 December 2022–1 January 2023.

5 *It is in the name of 'eternal Russia'* . . . : Ilya Budraitskis, 'Day 5, Day 9, Day 16: Responses to the Invasion of Ukraine', *London Review of Books*, Vol. 44, No. 6, 24 March 2022.

5 *Like warriors, what invading armies want, Weil writes* . . . : Simone Weil, 'The *Iliad*, or the Poem of Force', 1939, Simone Weil and Rachel Bespaloff, *War and the Iliad*, tr. Mary McCarthy (New York: New York Review of Books, 2005), 16.

7 *'When one of us dies, I will move to Paris'*: Sigmund Freud, 'Our Attitude Towards Death', Essay 1, *Thoughts for the Times on War and Death*, 1915, *The Standard Edition of the Complete Psychological Works* (London: Hogarth, Vol. 14, 1957), 298.

7–8 *'is for him to see that all the greed, aggression and deceit in the world* . . . ': D. W. Winnicott, 'Discussion of War Aims', *Home Is Where We Start From: Essays by a Psychoanalyst* (New York: Norton, 1986), 212.

10 *Consigning Covid to history, surveillance and testing capabilities have been dropped by countries across the world*: Philip Ball, 'Why are we pretending Covid's over?', *The Guardian*, 16 August 2022.

12 *This 'cold, virile' determination is rarely found, she suggested* . . . : Simone Weil quoted in Simone Pétrement, *Simone Weil: A Life* (New York: Pantheon, 1976), 375.

13 *was not 'kindled' by the desire to kill* . . . : Simone Weil quoted in Simone Pétrement, *Simone Weil: A Life*, 375.

13 *'might indeed have died at the very moment one is thinking about them* . . . *'*: Simone Weil, *Cahiers VI, Marseille*, Winter 1941–1942, in *Oeuvres complètes*, ed. Florence de Lussy (Paris: Gallimard, Quarto editions, 1999), 838.

13 *those who 'do not count', not 'in any situation, in anyone's eyes'*: Simone Weil, *La condition ouvrière* (Paris: Gallimard, 1951), 107, quoted in Simone Pétrement, *Simone Weil: A Life*, 245.

13 *Crucially, in the world of Homer, which was so important to Weil* . . . : For a fuller discussion of justice in relation to Homer, see Alasdair MacIntyre, *Whose Justice, Which Rationality* (London: Duckworth, 1988), 14.

14 *'more cruelly than water, earth, air and fire'; 'halted by the actual limits of the earth's surface'*: Simone Weil, 'Prospects—are we heading for the proletarian revolution?', 1933, *Oppression and Liberty*, tr. Arthur Wills and John Petrie (London: Routledge, 1958), 1, 19, 'Perspectives—Allons-nous vers la révolution prolétarienne', *Oeuvres complètes*, 268, 251.

14 *'stifle their own breath'; 'as safe as a little bird in front of a snake'*: Simone Weil, *The Need for Roots: Prelude to a Declaration of Duties Towards Mankind*, 1943, tr. Arthur Wills (London: Routledge, 1952), 28; 'L'enracinement', *Oeuvres complètes*, 1044.

14 *'as a child tearing the petals off a rose'*: Weil, *The Need for Roots*, 119; 'L'enracinement', *Oeuvres complètes*, 1101.

15 *'just as doctors are needed in a city stricken with plague'*: Simone Weil, 'Dernières Pensées', Letter to Father Perrin, Casablanca, 26 May 1942, *Oeuvres complètes*, 787.

15 *'they can'*: Tom Stevenson, 'Things fall from the sky', *London Review of Books*, Vol. 44, No. 7, 7 April 2022.

15 *'Each of us'*: Weil, *The Need for Roots*, 101, 'L'enracinement', *Oeuvres complètes*, 1089.

17 *'never, whatever may happen'*: Weil, 'The Causes of Liberty and Social Oppression', 1934, *Oppression and Liberty*, 'Réflexions sur les causes de la liberté et de l'oppression sociale', *Oeuvres complètes*, 79.

17 *Thought can be revolutionary or counter-revolutionary* . . . *'corrosive'*: Simone Weil, 'Fragments', *Oppression and Liberty*, 137, 'Méditation sur l'obéissance et la liberté', *Oeuvres complètes*, 493.

17 *'The powerful forces that we have to fight are preparing to crush us . . . '*: Simone Weil, 'Prospects', *Oppression and Liberty*, 22; 'Perspectives', *Oeuvres complètes*, 271.

17 *'nothing in the world can prevent us from thinking clearly'*; *'nothing can compel anyone to exercise their powers of thought . . . '*: Weil, 'Prospects', *Oppression and Liberty*, 22, 93; 'Perspectives', *Oeuvres complètes*, 271, 325.

19 *'The plague was unimaginable, or rather it was being imagined in the wrong way'*: Albert Camus, *La peste*, 1947, ed. W. J. Strachan (London: Methuen, 1962), 53; *The Plague*, tr. Stuart Gilbert (New York: Random House, 1948), 38 (some translations modified).

19 *'lacking in imagination . . . They don't think on the right scale for plagues . . . '*: Albert Camus, 'The composition of *The Plague*, from Notebooks II, III, and IV', *Selected Essays and Notebooks*, ed. and tr. Philip Thody (London: Hamish Hamilton, 1966), 228.

20 *'There have been as many plagues as wars in history . . . '*: Camus, *La peste*, 49; *The Plague*, 34.

20 *'It was only as time passed, and the rise in the steady death rate could not be ignored . . . '*: Camus, *La peste*, 93; *The Plague*, 72.

20 *'its self-command, the ruthless almost mathematical efficiency that had been its trump card hitherto'*: Camus, *La peste*, 290; *The Plague*, 242.

21 *'Counting' might, then, fall under the rubric of what Freud described . . . *: Sigmund Freud, 'The Antithetical Meaning of Primal Words', 1910, *Standard Edition*, Vol. 11 (London: Hogarth, 1957).

21 *'bedrooms, cellars, trunks, handkerchiefs and old papers . . . '*: Camus, *La peste*, 278; *The Plague*, 332.

21 *'It was as if the earth on which our houses were planted . . . '*: Camus, *La peste*, 26; *The Plague*, 15.

22 *In a 2020 interview, French analyst and theorist Julia Kristeva . . . *: Julia Kristeva, 'Humanity is rediscovering existential solitude, a sense of limits and of mortality', interview with Stefano Montefiore, *Corriera della Sera*, 29 March 2020, tr. into French by Henri José Legrand.

22 *'like a ghost that refused to depart for the other world'*: Lyra McKee, 'We were meant to be the generation that reaped the spoils of peace', *The Guardian*, 28 March 2020.

22 *'the days of young people disappearing and dying young would be gone'*: McKee, *The Guardian*, 2020.

22 *as if McKee had been warning us that we were about to enter, or re-enter, a state of war*: McKee, *The Guardian*, 2020.

23 *'the categorical refusal of an intrusion felt to be intolerable'*: Albert Camus, *L'homme révolté* (Paris: Gallimard, 1951), 21; *The Rebel*, tr. Anthony Bower, foreword by Sir Herbert Read (London: Hamish Hamilton, 1953), 19. My thanks to Neil Foxlee for his comments on the translation of Camus, see Letters, *London Review of Books*, Vol. 42, No. 10, 21 May 2020.

23 *'There are times when the only feeling I have is one of mad revolt . . . '*: Camus, *La peste*, 237–38; *The Plague*, 196-97.

24 *'The lockdown worked like a chemical experiment . . . '*: Arundhati Roy, 'The Pandemic Is a Portal', *Financial Times*, 3 April 2020.

25 *'could not understand how men could torture others while continuing to look at them'*: quoted by Olivier Todd in *Albert Camus: A Life* (London: Chatto and Windus, 1997), 313. N.B.: English translation gives quotes without references.

26 *'Our getting and spending . . . '*: Rebecca Solnit, 'Hope in a time of crisis', *The Guardian*, 7 April 2020.

26 *'Profiteers were taking a hand and purveying at enormous prices essential foodstuffs . . . '*: Camus, *La peste*, 258; *The Plague*, 214.

26 *'Thus whereas plague through its impartial ministrations should have promoted equality among our city's folk . . . '*: Camus, *La peste*, 258; *The Plague*, 214.

27 *'I thought, how could police use violence against the frontline fighters against Covid-19 . . . '*: Hannah Ellis-Petersen and Shah Meer-Baloch, 'Doctors tell of beatings by police amid ventilator and PPE shortage', *The Guardian*, 9 April 2020. See also Roy, 'The Pandemic Is a Portal'.

28 *There was an irony here*: See Jeremy Harding, 'The Castaway', *London Review of Books*, Vol. 36, No. 23, 4 December 2014.

28 *the 'institutional' injustice; the repeated 'lie' of assimilation . . .*: quoted by Morvan Lebesque in *Camus par lui-même*, 'Écrivains de toujours', 64 (Paris: Seuil, 1963), 125.

28 *a long extract of* The Plague *appeared clandestinely in France in a collection of Resistance publications*: Shoshana Felman, 'Camus' *The Plague*, or a Monument to Witnessing', Shoshana Felman and Dori Laub, *Testimony: Crises of Witnessing in Literature, Psychoanalysis and History* (New York: Routledge, 1992), 98.

29 *That epithet is reserved for the character of Joseph Grand for his acts of kindness and his dedication to an ideal . . .*: Camus, *La peste*, 57, 154; *The Plague*, 42, 126.

29 *'Evil sometimes has a human face . . .'*: Roland Barthes, *Bulletins du club du meilleur livre*, 1955, 7, quoted by Maciej Kałuża in 'The distance between reality and fiction: Roland Barthes reading Albert Camus', *Studia de Arte e Educacione*, 12, 2017.

29 *'no more than a puff of smoke'*; *'to die in heaps'*: Shoshana Felman, 'Camus' *The Plague*, or a Monument to Witnessing', 97. Camus, *La peste*, 50-51; *The Plague*, 35-36.

30 *'with genius added'*: Todd, *Albert Camus: A Life*, 168.

30 *'effacement'*; *'a motionless black figure which gradually merged into the invading darkness'*; *'only effacing herself a trifle more than usual'*: Camus, *La peste*, 298; *The Plague*, 248.

30 *The women in the novel are either patient sufferers, or occasional prophetesses . . .* : Camus, *La peste*, 297, 130; *The Plague*, 248, 104-105.

30 *'knew everything without ever thinking'*; *'the gift she had of knowing everything without apparently taking thought'*: Camus, *La peste*, 248; *The Plague*, 298.

31 *As the daily bombardment of numbers continued during Covid-19, one chilling statistic started to receive attention . . .* : Mark Townsend, 'Domestic violence cases soar as lockdown takes its toll', *The Guardian*, 4 April 2020; Anon, 'I know the trauma of domestic abuse. I fear for women in lockdown', *The Observer*, 12 April 2020.

32–33 *'Of course a man should fight for the victims. . . . but if that stops him from loving anything else, then what's the use of fighting?'*: Camus, *La peste*, 277; *The Plague*, 231.

33 *'Before them the darkness stretched out into infinity . . .'*: Camus, *La peste*, 277; *The Plague*, 232.

33 *The word comes close to the idea of calculated crime and from there to mass murder . . .* : Philippe Sands, *East West Street: On the origins of genocide and crimes against humanity* (London: Weidenfeld and Nicolson, 2016).

33 *For Tarrou, murder is state murder*: Camus, *La peste*, 266-75; *The Plague*, 222-30.

34 *'an accomplice'*: Camus, *La peste*, 176; *The Plague*, 215-16.

34 *'it desires to abolish it, but because it desires to monopolize it, like salt and tobacco'*: Sigmund Freud, 'The Disillusionment of the War', Essay 2, *Thoughts for the Times on War and Death*, 279.

35 *'quite simply what we learn in a time of pestilence: that there are more things to admire in men than to despise'*: Camus, *La peste*, 331; *The Plague*, 278.

37 *'is now perishing in the strife of nations'*: Freud to Jones, 25 December 1914, transcribed in Jones' hand, quoted by Peter Gay in *Freud: A Life For Our Time* (New York: Norton, 1988), 351.

37 *'I do not delude myself . . . The springtime of our science has abruptly broken off . . . '*: Freud to Jones, quoted in Gay, *Freud: A Life for Our Time*, 351.

37 *'unfolds one death at a time . . . '*: Rachel Clarke, 'Behind the statistics', *The Guardian*, 30 May 2020.

38 *'You have, my poor child, seen death break into the family for the first time, or heard about it . . . '*: Freud to Mathilda, 26 March 1908, Sigmund Freud, *Briefe 1873–1939* (Frankfurt: Fischer Verlag, 1960), 188; *Letters of Sigmund Freud*, ed. E. L. Freud, 137, quoted by Max Schur in *Freud: Living and Dying* (London: Hogarth Press and The Institute of Psychoanalysis, 1972), 263.

38 *In fact, according to some analysts, this was a fourth wave exclusive to northern countries, many of whose citizens had wrongly believed themselves to be free of the disease by December 1918 . . .* : Laura Spinney, *Pale Rider: The Spanish Flu of 1918 and How It Changed the World* (London: Vintage, 2017), 44-45.

38–39 *Things had started to go downhill for the Central Powers in April 1918 . . .* : Spinney, *Pale Rider*, 249-50.

39 *what can fairly be described as the worst 'massacre' of the twentieth century has been rubbed out of history*: Spinney, *Pale Rider*, 4.

39 *By autumn 1918, schools and theatres in the city were being intermittently closed . . .* : Gay, *Freud: A Life For Our Time*, 382.

39 *In May that year his wife, Martha, after years of undernourishment as she tried to manage caring for the whole family through the war . . .* : Gay, *Freud: A Life For Our Time*, 382.

39 *'a mutilated rump, bleeding from all arteries'*: Stefan Zweig, *Die Welt von Gestern, Erinnerungen eines Europäers* (1944), quoted in Gay, *Freud: A Life For Our Time*, 380.

39–40 *'I weep not a single tear for this Austria or this Germany'*: Zweig, *Die Welt von Gestern*, 256-59; Freud to Ferenczi, 23 August 1914, 25 October 1918, quoted by Ernest Jones in *Sigmund Freud: Life and Work*, Vol. 2, *Years of Maturity 1901–1919* (London: Hogarth, 1955), 192.

40 *'We are all of us slowly failing . . . '*: Freud to Jones, 15 January 1919, English Freud Collection, Library of Congress, quoted in Gay, *Freud: A Life For Our Time*, 378.

40 'Hungerkost': Freud to Ferenczi, 9 April 1919, quoted in Gay, *Freud: A Life For Our Time*, 381.

40 *'not even a children's train'*: Freud to Pfister, 27 January 1920, *Psychoanalysis and Faith: The Letters of Sigmund Freud and Oskar Pfister*, ed. Heinrich Meng and Ernst L. Freud, tr. Eric Mosbacher (London: Hogarth and the Institute of Psychoanalysis, 1963), 75.

40 *referring to the trains of the international children's association that were ferrying children out of starving Austria*: Schur, *Freud: Living and Dying*, 330.

40 *'prophetic dream'*: Freud to Ferenczi, 10 July 1915, quoted in Gay, *Freud: A Life For Our Time*, 354.

40 *More than a million Austro-Hungarian soldiers died either in battle or from disease*: Gay, *Freud: A Life For Our Time*, 381.

42 *'the perplexity and helplessness of the human race'*: Sigmund Freud, *The Future of an Illusion*, 1927, Vol. 21 (London: Hogarth, 1961), 18.

42 *'We are suffering under no restrictions, no epidemic, and are in good spirits'*: Freud to Jones, 22 October 1914, quoted in Gay, *Freud: A Life For Our Time*, 353.

42 *'my spirits are unshaken . . . '*: Freud to Ferenczi, 16 February 1917, quoted by Jones in *Sigmund Freud: Life and Work*, Vol. 2, 216.

42 *'join in the world's pleasure and the world's pain'*; 'der Erde Lust, der Erde Leid zu tragen': Freud to Abraham, 27 August 1918, quoted in Schur, *Freud: Living and Dying*, 316.

42 *'One has to use every means possible to withdraw from the frightful tension in the world outside . . . '*: Freud to Ferenczi, 2 August 1916, quoted in Jones, *Sigmund Freud: Life and Work*, 212.

42–43 *'I and my contemporaries will never again see a joyous world. It is too hideous'*: Freud to Lou Andreas-Salomé, quoted in Schur, *Freud: Living and Dying*, 292.

43 *'We have to abdicate . . . '*: Freud to Andreas-Salomé, quoted in Schur, *Freud: Living and Dying*, 292.

43 *he could not of course have foreseen today's Voluntary Human Extinction Movement . . .* : Sian Cain, 'Why a generation is choosing to be child-free', *The Guardian*, 25 July 2020.

43 *'perfection of the instruments of destruction'*; *'earlier periods of human arrogance had torn too wide apart between mankind and the animals'*: Freud, 'Why War?', 1933, *Standard Edition*, Vol. 22 (London: Hogarth, 1964), 213; *Moses and Monotheism*, 1939, *Standard Edition*, Vol. 23 (London: Hogarth, 1964), 100.

43 *'I myself was aware . . . '*: Freud to K. and L. Levy, 11 June 1923, quoted in Schur, *Freud: Living and Dying*, 358.

43 *'We shall remain inconsolable and never find a substitute . . . '*: Freud to Binswanger, 11–12 April 1929, quoted in Schur, *Freud: Living and Dying*, 421. Freud, 'Mourning and Melancholia', 1915, *Standard Edition*, Vol. 14 (London: Hogarth, 1957). Jeanne Wolff Bernstein, 'Spanish Flu, Covid-19 and Sigmund Freud: What can we learn from history', 3 September 2020 (Facebook and Freud Museum).

44 *'You will be able to certify that it was half-finished when Sophie was alive and flourishing'*: Freud to Max Eitingon, 18 July 1920, quoted in Schur, *Freud: Living and Dying*, 329, 553.

44 *'hitherto neglected and silent'*; *'rough-hewn and overwhelming'*: Ilse Grubrich-Simitis, *Back to Freud's Texts: Making Silent Documents Speak*, tr. Philip Slotkin (New Haven and London: Yale University Press, 1996), 1.

45 *Its only earlier appearance was in two letters to Eitingon of February 1920, just weeks after Sophie's death*: Grubrich-Simitis, *Back to Freud's Texts: Making Silent Documents Speak*, 189.

45 *'discussion concerning the mortality or immortality of protozoa'*: Grubrich-Simitis, *Back to Freud's Texts: Making Silent Documents Speak*, 189.

45 *'snatched away . . . as if she had never been'*: Freud to Pfister, 27 January 1920, *Psychoanalysis and Faith*, 75.

45 *'The undisguised brutality of our time . . . '*: Freud to Pfister, 27 January 1920, *Psychoanalysis and Faith*, 75.

46 This version of events is contested although there is no conclusive evidence for any of the alternative versions. For a strong summary of the issues, see Dany Nobus, 'Yom Kippur 1939: Freud, Schur and the Rupture of the Lethal Pact', *Freud in the Margins—Rethinking the History of Psychoanalysis* (New York, Columbia University Press, forthcoming); Michael Molnar, 'Death in the Library', unpublished manuscript. See also the letter from Lucie Freud to Felix Augenfeld, 2 October 1939, *Sigmund Freud Papers: Family Papers, 1851–1978; Correspondence between Others, 1870–1976*; Freud, Lucie; to Felix Augenfeld, 1939, 1973, 1976, Library of Congress. I am grateful to Daniela Finzi for alerting me to this controversy and to Dany Nobus and Michael Molnar for sharing their research.

47 '*If we are to die ourselves, and first to lose in death those who are dearest to us . . .* ': Sigmund Freud, *Beyond the Pleasure Principle*, 1920, *Standard Edition*, Vol. 18 (London: Hogarth, 1955), 45.

47 '*The aim of all life . . .* ': Freud, *Beyond the Pleasure Principle*, 38-39.

47–48 '*We are strengthened in our belief . . .* ': Freud, *Beyond the Pleasure Principle*, 45.

48 '*is often indistinguishable from deliberate destructiveness*': Zoe Williams, 'Isolating the over-50s? It's designed to sow discord', *The Guardian*, 4 August 2020.

49 '*easier to submit to a remorseless law of nature . . .*; 'Perhaps . . . we have adopted the belief because there is some comfort in it'; 'It may be . . . that this belief in the internal necessity of dying . . .* ': Freud, *Beyond the Pleasure Principle*, 45.

49 '*narcissistic injury*': Freud to Ferenczi, 4 February 1920, quoted in Schur, *Freud: Living and Dying*, 331.

49 '*I do as much work as I can . . .* ': Freud to Pfister, 27 January 1920, *Psychoanalysis and Faith*, 75.

50 '*melts away in their hands*': Freud, *Beyond the Pleasure Principle*, 45.

50 *death cannot be reduced to the appearance of a dead body, but describes the moment when a cell comes to the end of its individual development*: Freud, *Beyond the Pleasure Principle*, 45-49.

50 '*In this sense . . . protozoa too are mortal*': Freud, *Beyond the Pleasure Principle*, 47.

51–52 '*described repression, which lies at the basis of every neurosis, as a reaction to a trauma . . .* ': Sigmund Freud, Introduction to *Psychoanalysis and the War Neuroses*, 1919, *Standard Edition*, Vol. 17 (London: Hogarth, 1955), 210 (italics mine).

52 *By his own account, a traumatized soldier is torn between the two*: Freud, Introduction to *Psychoanalysis and the War Neuroses*, 209.

52 *I am referring to Freud's twelfth meta-psychological paper . . .* : Sigmund Freud, *A Phylogenetic Fantasy: Overview of the Transference Neuroses*, ed. and with an essay by Ilse Grubrich-Simitis, tr. Axel Hoffer and Peter T. Hoffer (Cambridge: Harvard University Press, 1987). Freud's title had been 'Overview of the Transference Neuroses', which Grubrich-Simitis makes the sub-title as it corresponds less closely to the work's content.

53 '*My thesis . . . is that Freud, in his phylogenetic fantasy . . .* ': Ilse Grubrich-Simitis, 'Trauma or drive—drive and Trauma: A Reading

of Sigmund Freud's *Phylogenetic Fantasy* of 1915', *The Psychoanalytic Study of the Child*, 43 (1988), 6.

53 *'the hitherto predominantly friendly outside world . . . transformed itself into a mass of threatening perils'*: Freud, *A Phylogenetic Fantasy: Overview of the Transference Neuroses*, 1915, 14.

53 *'Food was not sufficient to permit an increase in the human hordes . . . '*: Freud, *A Phylogenetic Fantasy: Overview of the Transference Neuroses*, 14.

53 *Faced with an emergency 'beyond his control', man imposed on himself a ban on reproduction . . .* : Freud, *A Phylogenetic Fantasy: Overview of the Transference Neuroses*, 15.

53 *'Language was magic to him, his thoughts seemed omnipotent to him, he understood the world according to his ego'*: Freud, *A Phylogenetic Fantasy: Overview of the Transference Neuroses*, 15.

54 *'The children bring along the anxiousness of the beginning of the Ice Age'*: Freud, *A Phylogenetic Fantasy: Overview of the Transference Neuroses*, 14.

54 *'preponderance of the phylogenetic disposition over all other factors'*: Freud, *A Phylogenetic Fantasy: Overview of the Transference Neuroses*, 14.

54 *'I have repeatedly been led to suspect that the psychology of the neuroses has stored up in it more of the antiquities of human development than any other source'*; *'many thousands of years'*: Sigmund Freud, 'The Paths to Symptom Formation', *Introductory Lectures on Psychoanalysis*, Part 3, Lecture 23, 1916–1917, *Standard Edition*, Vol. 16 (London: Hogarth, 1963), 371; *Totem and Taboo*, 1912–1913, *Standard Edition*, Vol. 13 (London: Hogarth, 1953), 158.

54 *'What . . . are the ways and means employed by one generation in order to hand on its mental states to the next one?'*: Freud, *Totem and Taboo*, 158.

55 *'It only moves it into still earlier prehistory'*: Freud, *A Phylogenetic Fantasy: Overview of the Transference Neuroses*, 10.

55 *'should we want to imagine a new man-made Ice Age, and think in psychoanalytic terms about the consequences of a nuclear winter'*: Grubrich-Simitis, 'Trauma or drive—drive or Trauma: A Reading of Sigmund Freud's *Phylogenetic Fantasy* of 1915', 5.

56 *'All our attention is directed to the outside, whence dangers threaten and satisfactions beckon . . . '*: Freud to Einstein, 26 March 1929, Library of Congress, quoted in Grubrich-Simitis (1996), 11, translation modified.

56 *'There is nothing for which man's capabilities are less suited . . .'*: Freud to Binswanger, 28 May 1911, quoted in Schur, *Freud: Living and Dying*, 262.

57 *'the claims of humanity'; 'the demands of a national war'*: Freud, *Psychoanalysis and the War Neuroses*, 214.

57 *'Consider . . . the Great War which is still laying Europe waste . . .'*: Sigmund Freud, *Introductory Lectures*, Part 2, Lecture 9, 'The Censorship of Dreams', *Standard Edition*, Vol. 15 (London: Hogarth, 1961), 146.

57 *'We lay a stronger emphasis on what is evil in men . . .'*: Freud, 'The Censorship of Dreams', 147.

58 *'In each of the loved persons . . . there was also something of the stranger . . .'*: Freud, 'Our Attitude Towards Death', *Thoughts for the Times on War and Death*, 293.

58 *'It was acquired . . . in relation to dead people who were loved as a reaction against the satisfaction hidden behind the grief for them . . .'*: Freud, 'Our Attitude Towards Death', 295.

58 *'vein of ethical sensitiveness'*: Freud, 'Our Attitude Towards Death', 295.

59 *'I, of course, belong to a race . . .'*: Freud to Romain Rolland, 8 April 1923, *Letters of Sigmund Freud*, ed. E. L. Freud, 200, quoted in Schur, *Freud: Living and Dying*, 350.

59 *Ten years later, in a letter to Marie Bonaparte, he predicted that persecution of the Jews and the suppression of intellectual freedom . . .*: Freud to Bonaparte, 26 March 1933, quoted in Schur, *Freud: Living and Dying*, 444.

59 *Although Freud remarked that the impulse to human empathy is difficult to explain, that compassion can be a veil for narcissism*: Sigmund Freud, *Group Psychology and the Analysis of the Ego* (1921), *Standard Edition*, Vol. 18 (London: Hogarth, 1955), 110n; *From the History of an Infantile Neurosis*, 1918, *Standard Edition*, Vol. 17 (London: Hogarth, 1955), 88.

59 *the protective shield of the psyche which allows itself to die to save the deeper layers of the mind from a similar fate . . .* : Freud, *Beyond the Pleasure Principle*, 27, 50.

60 *A life in which the pain of the times is shared, and in which every human subject, regardless of race, class, caste or sex would be able to participate*: Jacques Derrida, 'Spéculer sur Freud', *La carte postale, De Socrate à Freud et au-delà* (Paris: Flammarion, 1980), 288; on the concept of the 'commons' in time of pandemic, see also Etienne Balibar, 'On

living, learning, imagining in the middle of the crisis' [https://icls
.columbia.edu/etienne-balibar-on-living-learning-imagining-in-the
-middle-of-the-crisis/].

60 *'mysterious and beautiful book . . . '*: Theodor Reik, 'Introduction', Rachel Berdach, *The Emperor, the Sages and Death* (1938), tr. William Wolf, introd. by Theodor Reik (New York and London: Thomas Yoseloff, 1962), 8; Freud to Rachel Berdach, 27 December 1938, *Letters of Sigmund Freud*, quoted in Schur, *Freud: Living and Dying*, 514.

60 *'Who are you? . . . Where did you acquire all the knowledge expressed in your book?'*: Freud to Rachel Berdach, quoted in Schur, *Freud: Living and Dying*, 514.

61 *The psychoanalytic resonances are everywhere, from the emperor's wish to understand man's propensity for the dark . . .* : Berdach, *The Emperor, the Sages and Death*, 32, 90.

61 *'I wish to be conscious to the very end,' the emperor asserts, 'so as not to lose life's most mysterious part'*: Berdach, *The Emperor, the Sages and Death*, 142.

61 *'Is man alone accursed to know of death while full with life . . . '*: Berdach, *The Emperor, the Sages and Death*, 192.

62 *'My dream is this: not to be ruler in my land, in any land, neither be slave in any place, not to erect new boundaries . . . '*: Berdach, *The Emperor, the Sages and Death*, 127.

62 *'Whomever thou meetest, it is Thou . . . '*: Berdach, *The Emperor, the Sages and Death*, 168.

62 *A bit like the Freudian unconscious, this is a world that is both one and infinite, in which everything and everybody is included . . .* : Berdach, *The Emperor, the Sages and Death*, 189.

62 *But as we know, to die one's own death is not the same thing as to die alone in a world that seems deserted*: Haroon Siddique, 'Survivors of Covid-19 show increased rate of psychiatric disorders, study finds', *The Guardian*, 3 August 2020.

62 *'Cold fear now filled his heart. Where were the people, and was there war in the town? . . . '*: Berdach, *The Emperor, the Sages and Death*, 197.

63 *'Must he not share their fate before he dies?'*: Berdach, *The Emperor, the Sages and Death*, 196.

63 *'I say "my abominable fate", forgetting too quickly the millions of "abominable fates" being played out across Europe and everywhere without an end to blood . . . '*: 'In memoriam—Extraits du journal du Dr John Rittmeister, tenu en prison entre le 26 septembre 1942 et le 13

mai 1943', *Les années brunes—la psychanalyse sous le Troisième Reich* (Paris: Confrontation, 1984), 172.

64 *'love, not introversion'*: 'In memoriam—Extraits du journal du Dr John Rittmeister', *Les années brunes—la psychanalyse sous le Troisième Reich*, 174.

65 *'What did the "stay at home" message mean to you?' 'Death'*: 'Escaping My Abuser', *Panorama*, BBC, 17 August 2020.

66 *In the United States, women were prevented by their abusers from washing their hands*: See Andrew M. Campbell, 'Increasing Reports of Domestic Violence during the Covid-19 Pandemic', 'An Increasing Risk of Family Violence during the Covid-19 Pandemic: Strengthening Community Collaborations to Save Lives', *Forensic Science International Reports*, 12 April 2020 [https://www.ncbi.nlm.nih.gov /pmc/articles/PMC7152912/].

66 *In England, one couple sat listening to Boris Johnson on the radio when he announced the lockdown . . .* : 'Escaping My Abuser', *Panorama*, 17 August 2020.

67 *'shadow pandemic'*: United Nations, 'Policy Brief: The Impact of Covid-19 on Women', 9 April 2020 [www.un.org/sexualviolencein conflict/wp-content/uploads/2020/06/report/policy-brief-the-impact -of-covid-19-on-women/policy-brief-the-impact-of-covid-19-on -women-en-1.pdf]. Phumzile Mlambo-Ngcuka, Executive Director, UN Women, 'Violence against Women and Girls: The Shadow Pandemic', 6 April 2020 [www.unwomen.org/en/news/stories/2020/4 /statement-ed-phumzile-violence-against-women-during-pandemic].

67 *Visits to the website of Refuge, the United Kingdom's largest domestic-abuse charity, increased during the pandemic by over 60 per cent*: Mark Townsend, 'Revealed: surge in domestic violence during Covid-19 crisis', *The Guardian*, 12 April 2020. Gaby Hinsliff, 'The coronavirus backlash: how the pandemic is destroying women's rights', *The Guardian*, 23 June 2020. See also https://refuge.org.uk/wp-content /uploads/2021/03/Refuge-Covid-Service-Report.pdf, which gives the figure for April 2020 to February 2021 of an over 60 per cent increase of average calls and contacts on their data base compared with January to March 2020.

68 *According to the 'Counting Dead Women' campaign, during that time, sixteen women were murdered . . .* : Rachel Younger, 'Twice as many women killed by men during Covid Lockdown, charity reveals', 29 November 2020, ITV News [https://www.itv.com/news/2020-11-28

/three-times-more-women-killed-by-men-during-covid-lockdown
-charity-reveals]; Jamie Grierson, 'Domestic Abuse Killings "more
than double" amid Covid-19 lockdown', *The Guardian*, 15 April
2020 [https://www.theguardian.com/society/2020/apr/15/domestic
-abuse-killings-more-than-double-amid-covid-19-lockdown].

68 *'If you think it was bad before . . .* ': 'Escaping My Abuser', *Panorama*,
17 August 2020.

68 *Her partner boasted that he didn't have to 'cover up' any more while
repeatedly assuring her that she was safe at home . . .* : 'Escaping My
Abuser', *Panorama*, 17 August 2020.

68 *'It was at this moment she finally started to believe her partner would kill
her'*: Jamie Grierson, '"I live in fear of the unknown": Life in a Refuge
under Lockdown', *The Guardian*, 21 May 2020 [www.theguardian
.com/society/2020/may/21/i-live-in-fear-of-the-unknown-life-in-a
-refuge-under-lockdown].

68 *With reference to Covid-19, Julia Kristeva uses the term 'feminicide' . . .* : Julia Kristeva, 'La situation virale et ses résonances psycha-
nalytiques', webinar, 14 June 2020 [www.ipa.world/IPA/en/IPA1/
Webinars/La_situation_virale.aspx]. On femicide, see Diana E. H.
Russell and Nicole Van de Ven, *Crimes against Women: Proceedings of
the International Tribunal* (Millbrae, CA: Les Femmes, 1976).

69 *As defences start to crumble, the phobic core of being human explodes*: As
Andrea Long Chu points out, women are being assaulted by men for
whom being confined at home risks turning them into women. See
Long Chu, *Females* (London and New York: Verso, 2019).

69 *Domestic violence has become more visible, but the renewed attention
has not reduced the prevalence of sexual crime—if anything the opposite*:
Rajeev Sayal and Alexandra Topping, 'Plan to tackle sexual assault a
"pipe dream" as offences hit a record high', *The Guardian*, 29 April
2022.

70 *'With the schools closed . . . 45 per cent of men say they are spending more
time home-schooling than their wives'*: Eliot Weinberger, 'The American Virus', *London Review of Books*, Vol. 42, No. 11, 4 June 2020.

71 *Angela Merkel warned of a creeping 'retraditionalization' of roles*: Angela
Merkel, quoted by Rory Carroll, Kate Connolly, Ashifa Kassam and
Kim Willsher in '"We are losers in this crisis": research finds lockdowns
reinforcing gender inequality', *The Guardian*, 29 May 2020 [www.
theguardian.com/global-development/2020/may/29/we-are-losers-in
-this-crisis-research-finds-lockdowns-reinforcing-gender-inequality].

71 *The domestic workload of women in France tripled between March and May 2020*: Carroll, Connolly, Kassam and Willsher, '"We are losers in this crisis": research finds lockdowns reinforcing gender inequality', *The Guardian*, 29 May 2020.

71 *In Spain, more than 170,000 people signed a petition protesting against this 'regression'*: Carroll, Connolly, Kassam and Willsher, '"We are losers in this crisis": research finds lockdowns reinforcing gender inequality', *The Guardian*, 29 May 2020.

71 *In the United Kingdom, the 'early years' sector has been pushed to the brink of collapse* . . . : Hinsliff, 'The coronavirus backlash: how the pandemic is destroying women's rights', *The Guardian*, 23 June 2020.

71 *According to the British campaign group Pregnant Then Screwed, more than half of pregnant women and mothers expected the pandemic permanently to damage their careers*: Hinsliff, 'The coronavirus backlash: how the pandemic is destroying women's rights', *The Guardian*, 23 June 2020.

71 *the countries that dealt better with Covid-19, at least at the outset, were all led by women* . . . : See Jon Henley, 'Female-led countries handled Covid-19 better, research finds', *The Guardian*, 19 August 2020 [www.theguardian.com/world/2020/aug/18/female-led-countries-handled-coronavirus-better-study-jacinda-ardern-angela-merkel]; Judy Stober, Letters, *The Guardian*, 25 August 2020 [www.theguardian.com/world/2020/aug/24/women-excel-in-handling-covid-19]. See also Jacqueline Rose, 'Afterword', *On Violence and On Violence Against Women* (New York: Farrar, Straus and Giroux; London: Faber, 2021).

71–72 *We might, for example, contrast Johnson's avoidance of the families of the bereaved with Jacinda Ardern's physical embrace of the survivors of the Christchurch mosque massacre in 2019* . . . ; *Or we might note how Mia Mottley's handling of the pandemic more or less coincided with the transition of Barbados to a republic* . . . : Nesrine Malik, 'With respect: how Jacinda Ardern showed the world what a world leader should be', *The Guardian*, 19 March 2019; Alice Scarsi, 'Queen heartbreak as Barbados Prime Minister launches COP26 speech after republican vow', *Daily Express*, 1 November 2021.

72 *'The evolution of civilization* . . . *'*: Sigmund Freud, *Civilization and its Discontents*, 1930, *Standard Edition*, Vol. 21 (London: Hogarth, 1961), 122.

72 *which is why Freud could also assert without contradiction that the human organism wants above all to die after its own fashion*: Freud, *Beyond the Pleasure Principle*, 39.

74 *'fluctuating, vague and uncertain . . .'; 'The senses in which I am using the term [uncertain] . . . is that in which the prospect of a European war is uncertain . . . '*: John Maynard Keynes, 'The General Theory of Employment, Interest, and Money', 1937, *The Collected Writings of John Maynard Keynes*, Vol. 14 (Macmillan: Cambridge University Press for the Royal Economic Society, 1973), 113.

76 *Freud once stated that no one believes in their own death*: Freud, 'Our Attitude Towards Death', 289.

77 *'There used to be no house, hardly a room, in which someone had not once died'*: Walter Benjamin, 'The Storyteller', *Illuminations*, ed. Hannah Arendt, tr. Harry Zohn (London: Fontana, 1973), 94.

79 *'We were terrified of this new disease . . . '*: quoted by Oliver Franklin-Wallace in 'An oral history of AstraZeneca: "Making a vaccine in a year is like landing on the moon"', *The Guardian*, 28 August 2021.

79 *'Expansion is everything . . . '*: quoted by Hannah Arendt, *The Origins of Totalitarianism*, 1951, (New York: Harcourt, Brace, Jovanovich, 1979), 124.

80 *Rhodes' statue at the University of Cape Town was brought down by student protests in one of the most resonant political actions of the times . . .*: I discuss the 'Rhodes Must Fall' campaign in South Africa more fully in 'Political Protest and the Denial of History—South Africa and the Legacy of the Future', *On Violence and On Violence Against Women*.

80 *'We know there is life on Mars . . . because we sent it there'*: quoted by Nicola Twilly in 'Meet the Martians', *New Yorker*, 8 October 2015.

80 *'We've got a lot of land with nobody around, so if it blows up, it's cool . . . '*: Elon Musk, quoted by Dianna Wray in 'Elon Musk SpaceX Launch site threatens wildlife in Texas, environmental groups say', *The Guardian*, 5 September 2021.

81 *The British psychoanalyst D. W. Winnicott, writing in 1949, described a patient who had to go looking for a piece of their past in the future . . .*: D. W. Winnicott, 'Fear of Breakdown', *International Review of Psychoanalysis*, 1974.

81 *The first hysterical patient in the history of psychoanalysis—analyzed by Freud's colleague Josef Breuer—fell ill as she sat nursing her dying father . . .*: Freud and Josef Breuer, 'Anna O', *Studies on Hysteria*, 1893–1895, *Standard Edition*, Vol. 2 (London: Hogarth, 1955).

82 *When you are grieving there is nothing else to do but grieve, as the mind battles against a knowledge which no one ever wishes to own*: Denise Riley, *Say Something Back—Time Lived Without its Flow* (London: PanMacmillan, 2016).

83 *'I will never forget the pain of the children running down the hospital corridor . . . and having to leave again'*: Tatler Archive, 'Boris Johnson's mother on her soft-hearted son', *Tatler*, 14 September 2021.

84 *When a group of British Airways passengers and crew, who had been taken hostage and held as human shields by Saddam Hussein in 1990 at the start of the Gulf War . . .*: Mike White, 'The Awful Secret of Flight 149: Spies, Lies and Ruined Lives', *Stuff*, 8 August 2021 [https://www.stuff.co.nz/entertainment/books/125874638/the-awful-secret-of-flight-149-spies-lies-and-ruined-lives].

85 *forty years after the scandal, in August 2022, interim payments were announced for the survivors, but thousands of the parents and children of victims have still received nothing*: Matthew White, 'Survivors of contaminated blood scandal awarded interim payments', *The Guardian*, 17 August 2022.

85 *'manufacturing offences from the past'*: Tom Wilkinson, 'Under-fire Education Secretary calls on universities to bring nation together', *Evening Standard*, 9 September 2021.

86 *'My terror of forgetting . . . is greater than my terror of having too much to remember'*: Yosef Hayim Yerushalmi, *Zakhor—Jewish History and Jewish Memory* (Seattle: University of Washington Press, 1996), 117.

87 *Squabbling over whether the US is a 'big' or 'super' power—according to Ben Wallace, UK Defence Minister at the time . . .*: Dan Sabbagh and Patrick Wintour, 'UK defence secretary suggests US is no longer a superpower', *The Guardian*, 2 September 2021.

88 *'left just to be and then gradually disappear. To have its quietness'*: quoted by Charlotte Higgins, 'Rachel Whiteread: "I wanted to make the opposite of what I had always been making"': *The Guardian*, 12 April 2021.

89 *'For some years . . . I have held the theory that joy is an indispensable ingredient in human life, for the health of the mind'; 'equivalent of madness'*: Simone Weil, Letter to Jean Posternak, 1938, *Seventy Letters—Personal and Intellectual Windows on a Thinker*, tr. and arr. by Richard Rees (Eugene, Oregon: Wipf and Stock, 1965), 95.

90 *'the nationalist obsession, the adoration of power in its most brutal form . . .'*: Weil, Spring 1937, *Seventy Letters*, 84.

91 *'morally unbreathable atmosphere'; 'intoxicated'; 'both of terror and love to the whole universe'*: Weil, *Seventy Letters*, 94.

91 *'An incredible amount of lying, false information, demagogy, mixed boastfulness and panic'*: Weil, *Seventy Letters*, 94.

91 *She could be describing the UK in the throes of Brexit, or the US, faced with the ascendancy of China . . .* : Weil, *Seventy Letters*, 94.

91 *'Freedom, justice, art, thought and similar kinds of greatness'*: Weil, *Seventy Letters*, 94.

91 *'French sanity . . . is becoming endangered. To say nothing of the rest of Europe'*: Weil, *Seventy Letters*, 95.

91 *'Why . . . have I not the infinite number of existences I need?'*: Weil, Letter to Posternak, quoted in Pétrement, *Simone Weil: A Life*, 315.

92 *'so sculptural'*: Weil, Letter to Posternak, quoted in Pétrement, *Simone Weil: A Life*, 315 (translation modified).

92 *Weil's mother told her that killing to prevent a rape was the one exception she made to the commandment that one should not kill*: Pétrement, *Simone Weil: A Life*, 193.

92 *'upsurge'*: Simone Weil, 'La personne et le sacré—Collectivité, Personne, Impersonnel, Droit, Justice', 1943, *Écrits de Londres et dernières lettres*, 23, originally published as 'The Fallacy of Personal Rights', *Twentieth Century*, May and June, 1959.

92 *Antigone in particular she returned to at the end of her life . . .* : Weil, 'La personne et le sacré', *Écrits de Londres et dernières lettres*, 23.

92 *'They contented themselves with the name of justice'*: Weil, 'La personne et le sacré', *Écrits de Londres et dernières lettres*, 23.

92–93 *'consecrated'; 'surely guarantee her a place in the first rank'; 'stubbornly refused'; 'ersatz of grandeur'; 'sought to conquer nothing'*: Albert Camus, *Nouvelle revue française*, June 1949, 'Commentaires'; Weil, *Oeuvres complètes*, 1264.

93 *'the sole great thinker of her time'*: Albert Camus to Selma Weil, 11 February 1951, 'Vie et oeuvres', *Oeuvres complètes*, 91.

93 *'terrible and pitiless in its audacity'; 'rare heights of thought'*: Camus quoted in opening 'Presentation' of Weil, *L'enracinement*, ed. Florence de Lussy and Michael Narcy (Paris: Flammarion, 2014), 55.

93 *'This does not distress me at all'*: Weil, Letter to her parents, 18 July 1943, *Seventy Letters*, 196–97.

94 *'Hope . . . but in moderation'*: Weil, Letter to her parents, 4 July 1943, *Oeuvres complètes*, 1237.

94 *'You have . . . bequeathed these ruined faces to me'*: Sylvie Weil, *At Home with André and Simone Weil*, tr. Benjamin Ivry (Illinois: Northwestern University Press, 2010), 114.

95 *'Simone . . . had already been transformed into a saint, and Selma into the saint's mother'*: Sylvie Weil, *At Home with André and Simone Weil*, 98-100.

95 *There is no unifying thread through the writings of Simone Weil, and any attempt to create one risks compartmentalizing her ideas, creating false distinctions and separations*: A short version of this chapter was originally published as a review of Robert Zaretsky, *The Subversive Simone Weil: A Life in Five Ideas* (Chicago: University of Chicago Press, 2021).

95–96 *As if, Weil wrote, someone were endlessly whispering in your ear, 'You are nothing,' 'You do not count.' 'You are here to bend, to submit, to shut up'*: Weil, 'The *Iliad*, or the Poem of Force', 5.

96 *She also lost her faith in any version of politics grounded in parties and trade unions*: On Weil's vexed relationship to her own Jewishness, see Thomas R. Nevin, *Simone Weil: Portrait of a Self-Exiled Jew* (Chapel Hill: University of North Carolina Press, 1991). Florence de Lussy, 'Excès et errements' and 'Un rejet du judaïsme', *Simone Weil, Que sais-je?* (Paris: Editions poches, 2021). My thanks to Florence de Lussy for sharing this work with me. Gillian Rose, 'Angry Angels: Simone Weil and Emmanuel Levinas', *Judaism and Modernity: Philosophical Essays* (Oxford: Blackwells, 1993).

96 *'The Christian (by instinct if not by baptism) who, in 1943, died in a London hospital because she would not eat "more than her ration . . ."'*: Anne Reynaud-Guérithault, 'Introduction', Weil, *Lectures on Philosophy*, tr. Hugh Price, 1933–1934 (Cambridge: Cambridge University Press, 1978), 25.

97 *'Only if you believe your place is on the lowest rung of the ladder . . . will you be led to regard others as your equal rather than giving preference to yourself'*: Weil, *Cahiers VI*, 860.

97 *'is the situation of those who find themselves at the rear'*: Weil, Letter to Georges Bernanos, 1938, *Oeuvres complètes*, 406, 15n8.

97 *At eleven years old, living in Paris, she had joined a demonstration of workers demanding shorter hours and higher wages . . .* : Pétrement, *Simone Weil: A Life*, 20.

98 *'forthrightness'*; *'simpering graces'*; *'Your son, Simon'*: Pétrement, *Simone Weil: A Life*, 28. Sylvie Weil, *At Home with André and Simone Weil*, 62, 107.

98 *'André . . . never described his sister as a woman . . .* ': Sylvie Weil, *At Home with André and Simone Weil*, 62.

98 *'I beg you . . . to protect her from exchanging smiles with admirers! I assure you that her personality is already starting to form*': Weil, Letter to Selma Weil, quoted in Sylvie Weil, *At Home with André and Simone Weil*, 109.

98 *'being wasted by sterile chagrin*': Weil, *Seventy Letters*, 156.

99 *'I envied her . . . for having a heart that could beat right across the world*': quoted in Pétrement, *Simone Weil: A Life*, 51.

99 *Struck low by repeated rejection, she felt that she risked dying of grief . . .* : Pétrement, *Simone Weil: A Life*, 533.

99 *According to Simone Pétrement, none of those who were with her in London . . .* : Pétrement, *Simone Weil: A Life*, 526.

99 *'Everyone . . . commands wherever he has the power to do so*': Weil, 'Luttons-nous pour la justice?', 1957, *Écrits de Londres et dernières lettres*, 20.

100 *'The true God is God conceived as almighty, but as not commanding everywhere he could*'; *'the universe into existence by consenting not to command it*': Simone Weil, 'Forms of the Implicit Love of God', *Waiting for God*, 1942, tr. Emma Craufurd (New York: Harper, 1973), 144, 158. Weil, 'Formes de l'amour implicates de Dieu', *Oeuvres complètes*, 723, 731.

100 *'as sovereign*': Weil, *Cahiers VI*, 907.

100 *'the rich are invincibly led to believe they are someone*': Weil, *Cahiers VI*, 901.

100–101 *'It is perfectly fine that you lack the privileges I possess*'; *'I claim for each and every one of you an equal share in the privileges I myself enjoy*': Weil, 'La personne et le sacré,' *Écrits de Londres et dernières lettres*, 26.

101–102 *'The dark night of God's absence is itself the soul's contact with God*'; *'cords that attach us to the world to break*'; *'logical to the bitter end*': Susan Taubes, 'The Absent God', *The Journal of Religion*, Vol. 35, No. 1, January 1955.

102 *'both in my intellect and in the centre of my heart*': Weil, *Seventy Letters*, 178.

102 *'I am not the maiden who awaits her betrothed but the unwelcome third*'; *'I love you. I love you. I love you*': Weil, *Cahiers III*, 926.

102 *'profoundly tricky spiritual fact, viz that I cannot go towards God in love without bringing myself along*': Anne Carson, *Decreation: Poetry, Essays, Opera* (New York: Vintage, 2005), 168-69.

103 *Although in her notebooks she dismissed the inner life as 'temptation',* *she was an astute reader of his ideas*: quoted by Robert Esposito in *The Origin of the Political: Hannah Arendt or Simone Weil* (New York: Fordham University Press, 2017), 81n.

103 *'thoughts we do not think, wishes we do not wish in our soul'*; *'wooden horses in which there are warriors leading an independent life'*: Weil, *Lectures in Philosophy*, 93-94, 97.

103 *'Are there really in our souls . . . thoughts which escape us?'*: Weil, *Lectures in Philosophy*, 94.

103 *'What we believe to be our ego* (moi)*. . . is as fugitive as a wave on the sea'*: Weil, 'L'amour de Dieu et le malheur', 1942, *Oeuvres complètes*, 708.

103 *'If we are to perish . . . let us see to it that we do not perish without having existed'*: Weil, 'Prospects', *Oppression and Liberty*, 22; 'Perspectives', *Oeuvres complètes*, 271.

103 *'dark ideas'; 'brilliant self-assertiveness of her writerly project?'; 'The answer is we can't'*: Carson, *Decreation: Poetry, Essays, Opera*, 171.

104 *'What we see so hideously before us are our own traits, only enlarged. This thought must not be allowed, far from it, to reduce by one jot our energy for the struggle'*: Weil, 'Cette guerre est une guerre de réligions', *Écrits de Londres et dernières lettres*, 91.

104 *'It is often said that force is powerless to overcome thought . . . but for this to be true there must be thought'*: Weil, 'Reflections on the Causes of Liberty and Social Oppression', *Oppression and Liberty*, 112, 'Réflexions sur les causes de la liberté et de l'oppression sociale,' *Oeuvres complètes*, 343.

104 *Likewise, her strongest indictment of factory piece-work stemmed from the way it robbed the worker of any time or space for thought . . .* : Weil, 'Factory Work', tr. Felix Giovanelli, *Politics*, December 1946, 372, 'Expérience de la vie d'usine', *Oeuvres complètes*, 201.

104 *'excludes all rules and predictions'*: Weil, 'Factory Work', 375, 'Expérience de la vie d'usine', *Oeuvres complètes*, 208.

104 *Anything less, she insisted, and life becomes uninhabitable, impossible to breathe*: Weil, 'Factory Work', 375, 'Expérience de la vie d'usine', *Oeuvres complètes*, 208.

104–105 *'I do not recognize . . . any right on the part of the Church to limit the workings of the intellect . . . '*: Weil, *Pensées sans ordre concernant l'amour de Dieu*, quoted in Pétrement, *Simone Weil: A Life*, 523.

105 'anathema sit': Weil, 'Autobiographie spirituelle: Letter to Father Perrin', 15 May 1942, *Oeuvres complètes*, 779.

105 *She refused to be baptized*: This has been disputed. For a summary
of the evidence and arguments both ways, see Eric Springsted,
'Simone Weil and Baptism' [http://www.laici.va/content/dam/laici
/documenti/donna/culturasocieta/english/simone-weil-and-baptism
.pdf].

105 '*by them alone*'; '*unique and perpetual obligation*'; '*all privations of the
soul and of the body likely to destroy or mutilate the earthly life of any
human being whoever they may be*': Weil, 'Étude pour une Déclaration
des Obligations Envers l'être humain', *Écrits de Londres et dernières
lettres*, 66-71; tr. Richard Rees, 'Draft for a Statement of Human
Obligations', *Two Moral Essays*, ed. Robert Hathaway, Pendle Hill,
1981.

106 '*a form of justice, a way of restoring balance*': Sylvie Weil, *At Home with
André and Simone Weil*, 150.

106 '*You are doing what my sister would have done . . . because she was
honest, by and large*': Sylvie Weil, *At Home with André and Simone
Weil*, 171.

106 '*entwined*': See Gillian Rose, 'Angry Angels', *Judaism and Modernity:
Philosophical Essays* (Oxford: Blackwells, 1993).

107 '*As soon as any category of humans is placed outside the pale of those
whose life has value, nothing is more natural than to kill them*': Weil,
Introduction, 'Une anarchiste en espagne', 1936–1938, *Oeuvres complètes*, 390-91.

108 '*serious wound*': Weil, 'Une anarchiste en espagne', *Oeuvres complètes*,
390-91.

108 '*astonished I didn't laugh*': Weil, Letter to Georges Bernanos, 1938,
Oeuvres complètes, 407.

108 '*Not once have I seen anyone . . .* ': Weil, Letter to Georges Bernanos,
Oeuvres complètes, 408.

108 '*You are . . . the only person, to my knowledge . . .* ': Weil, Letter to
Georges Bernanos, *Oeuvres complètes*, 409.

108 '*The desire to humiliate the enemy . . .* ': Weil, Letter to Georges
Bernanos, *Oeuvres complètes*, 409.

108 '*exaltation of a kid caught up in a war*': Weil, Letter to Georges Bernanos, *Oeuvres complètes*, 409.

108 '*I must confess . . . that to my way of feeling, there would be less shame
for France . . .* ': quoted in Pétrement, *Simone Weil: A Life*, 327.

109 '*carving out for herself her share of black or yellow human flesh*': Weil,
The Need for Roots, 195; 'L'enracinement', *Oeuvres complètes*, 1149.

109 *'I cannot complain . . . that we are suffering the fate that we have inflicted on others'*: Weil, 'A propos de la question colonial dans ses rapports avec le destin du peuple français', 1943, *Oeuvres complètes*, 431.

109 *But she was right that a democracy made up of opposing parties had been powerless to prevent the formation of a party . . .*: Weil, *The Need for Roots*, 28, 'L'enracinement', *Oeuvres complètes*, 1044.

110 *'is that, as a general rule, a people's generosity rarely extends to making the effort to uncover the injustices committed in their name'*: Weil, 'Les Nouvelles données du problème colonial dans l'empire français', 1938, *Oeuvres complètes*, 420.

110 *'In so far as we register the evil and ugliness within us . . .'*: Weil, 'Forms of the Implicit Love of God', *Waiting for God*, 190 (translation modified), 'Formes de l'amour implicite de Dieu', 1942, *L'attente de Dieu, Oeuvres complètes*, 749.

111 *She also found herself wanting to hit other people on the head*: Weil, *Cahiers VI*, 832, 836.

111 *'norm and aim of life'*: Weil, 'Autobiographie spirituelle', *Oeuvres complètes*, 768.

111 *'with all one's soul'; 'mere fragment of living matter'*: Weil, 'L'amour de Dieu et le malheur', *Cahiers VI*, 710, 857.

112 *Unlike the Roman Empire whose spirit he inherited . . .* : Weil, 'Les origines de l'Hitlerisme', 1940, *Oeuvres complètes*, 377.

112 *'The victory of those defending by means of arms a just cause, is not necessarily . . . a just victory'; 'allowing that this is our destiny'; 'accept for themselves the transformation they would have imposed on the vanquished'*: Weil, 'Les origines de l'Hitlerisme', *Oeuvres complètes*, 377.

112 *'the purest triumph of love, the crowning grace of war . . . '*: Weil, 'The Iliad, or the Poem of Force', 29.

112 *Weil calls for people from different stations in life, different nations . . .* : Weil, 'The Iliad, or the Poem of Force', 14, 35.

113 *You are turning disgust into a willing and tender embrace*: Weil, 'L'amour de Dieu et le malheur', *Oeuvres complètes*, 710.

113 *'It is as easy . . . to direct the mind willingly towards affliction as it is for a dog . . . '*: Weil, 'Lettre à Joë Bousquet', 12 May 1942, *Oeuvres complètes*, 794.

113 *'upsurge' . . . 'transports'*: Weil, 'Forms of the Implicit Love of God', 146-47; 'Formes de l'amour implicite de Dieu,' *Oeuvres complètes*, 724.

113 *In the final analysis, with the odds piled against it . . .* : Weil, *Cahiers VI*, 857.

114 *'You do not have the same reasons as I have . . . to feel hatred and revulsion towards me'*; *'It is not by chance . . . that you have never been loved'*: Simone Weil, *First and Last Notebooks*, ed. and tr. Richard Rees (New York: OUP, 1970), 43.

114 *'the colour of a dead leaf, like certain insects'*: Weil, 'Autobiographie spirituelle', *Oeuvres complètes*, 770, 766, 775, 788.

114 *'malcontents'*: Weil, quoted in Pétrement, *Simone Weil: A Life*, 236.

115 *'sole guide'*: Weil, 'Réflexions en vue d'un bilan', 1939, *Oeuvres complètes*, 519.

115 *Elsewhere, a dog barking beside the prostrate body of his master lying dead in the snow . . .*: Weil, 'La personne et le sacré', *Écrits de Londres et dernières lettres*, 34.

115 *Skin peeled from a burning object it has stuck to . . .*: Weil, *The Need for Roots*, 157, 'L'enracinement', *Oeuvres complètes*, 1126.

115 *'a child without meat asking for salt'*: Weil, *The Need for Roots*, 32, 'L'enracinement', *Oeuvres complètes*, 1047.

115 *'the child about to be born in the making of the layette'*: Weil, *The Need for Roots*, 95, 'L'enracinement', *Oeuvres complètes*, 1085.

115 *Nothing exists, Weil states, without its analogy in numbers*: Weil, 'Letter to André Weil', *Oeuvres complètes*, 569.

115 *God loves, not as I love, but as an emerald 'is' green*: Weil, *Cahiers III*, 926.

115 *'are the only characters to speak the truth'*; *'Can't you see the affinity, the essential analogy between these fools and me?'*: Weil to her parents, 4 August 1943, *Oeuvres complètes*, 1236.

115 *'analogy and transference'*: Weil, 'Forms of the Implicit Love of God', 184, 'Formes de l'amour implicite de Dieu', *Oeuvres complètes*, 746.

116 *it is a miracle, she insists, that thoughts are expressible given the myriad combinations which they make*: Weil, 'La personne et le sacré', *Écrits de Londres*, 30-31.

117 *'the same state of grave disorder as the language of natural science in the imaginary world I have just described'*: Alasdair MacIntyre, *After Virtue: A Study in Moral Theory* (London: Duckworth, 1981), 2.

119 *In November 2022, it emerged that the richest nations, notably the US, UK, Canada and Australia . . .*: Damian Carrington, 'Revealed: US and UK fall billions short of "fair share" of climate funding', *The Guardian*, 7 November 2022.

119 *'We were the ones whose blood, sweat and tears financed the industrial revolution . . .'*: Damian Carrington, Patrick Greenfield, Fiona Har-

vey, Nina Lakhani, 'Barbados PM launches blistering attack on rich nations at COP27 climate talks', *The Guardian*, 7 November 2022.

119 *'According to the UN Secretary General, António Guterres . . . '*: Damian Carrington, '"Climate carnage": UN demands funding surge to save millions of lives', *The Guardian*, 3 November 2022.

121 *One unregulated digital ad in the November 2022 US mid-term elections used a horror movie soundtrack punctuated by gunfire . . .* : Ed Pilkington, 'Political messaging—Unregulated, highly targeted digital ads eclipse old media', *The Guardian*, 4 November 2022.

122 *'Let there be no talk of "mental illness . . ."'*: Jeff Sharlet quoted in Eyal Press, 'Power, politics and feelings—whether it's the courtroom or the waiting room, it's impossible to take politics out of mental health', *The New York Times, Sunday Opinion*, 16 October 2022.

122 *'all the social trappings of civilized society'; 'shockingly easy'; 'How many wars are morally unambiguous?'*: Jeffrey Gettleman, 'American Finds in Ukraine the War He Sought', *The New York Times*, 10 October 2022.

123 *'an exogamous, extreme event'*: Peter Walker, 'Kwarteng: even more tax cuts to come and fewer regulations', *The Guardian*, 26 September 2022.

124 *Courage can sustain injustice . . .* : MacIntyre, *After Virtue: A Study in Moral Theory*, 200.

124 *'lives again in the capitalists who, to maintain their privileges, acquiesce light-heartedly in the wars that may rob them of their sons'*: Weil, 'Reflections', *Oppression and Liberty*, 64, 'Réflexions', *Oeuvres complètes*, 301.

125 *He was warning against the risks of invoking the hidden depths of psychic life in the courtroom . . .* : Sigmund Freud, 'Dostoevsky and Parricide,' 1928, *Standard Edition*, Vol. 21 (London: Hogarth, 1961), 189. The phrase is Constance Garnet's in her translation from the German which has 'a stick with two ends'.

125 *'were neither good nor bad'*: Sigmund Freud, 'The Disillusion of the War', *Thoughts for the Times on War and Death*, 281.

125 *'The word traitor . . . should only be used about those of whom one feels certain . . . '*: Weil to Jean Wahl, New York, 1942, *Seventy Letters*, 158-59.

125 *'who desired it emotionally and who welcomed it when it was done'*: Freud, 'Dostoevsky and Parricide', 189.

126 *'an uninterrupted battle directed mainly against herself'*: Roberto Esposito, *The Origin of the Political: Hannah Arendt or Simone Weil?*,

tr. Vincenzo Binetti and Gareth Williams (New York: Fordham University Press, 2017), 69.

126 'torn heart'; 'extreme discord': Esposito, *The Origin of the Political: Hannah Arendt or Simone Weil?*, 5.

126 'to kill as little as possible': *The Notebooks of Simone Weil*, tr. Arthur Wills (New York: Routledge, 2004), quoted in Esposito, *The Origin of the Political: Hannah Arendt or Simone Weil?*, 5.

126 'obliterates anybody who feels its touch': Weil, 'The *Iliad*, or the Poem of Force', 20.

126 'triumph of love'; 'crowning grace': Weil, 'The *Iliad*, or the Poem of Force', 29.

126 *It was, therefore, a central component of Aristotelian virtue to give death and human vulnerability their due*: MacIntyre, *After Virtue: A Study in Moral Theory*, 128-29.

127 'May I be alive when I die': 'D. W. W.: A Reflection', in D. W. Winnicott, *Psycho-Analytic Explorations*, ed. Clare Winnicott, Ray Shepherd, Madeleine Davis (London: Karnac Books, 1989), 4.

127 'I do not know . . . why a curious division of labour prevails': Judith N. Shklar, *The Faces of Injustice* (New Haven: Yale University Press, 1990), 16.

128 *It is not often that a story of war, whether as fiction or non-fiction, is told through the eyes of women*: Svetlana Alexievich, *The Unwomanly Face of War* (1985), tr. Richard Pevear and Larissa Volokhonsky (London: Penguin Random House, 2017) (first uncensored version). The book was unpublished for two years after completion because it went against the Russian history of the war.

128 'Something unknown to her had entered her flesh like fire': Alberto Moravia, *Two Women*, 1957, tr. Angus Davidson (London: Secker and Warburg, 1958), 322.

128 'I'm going to kill you': Moravia, *Two Women*, 317.

129 'You were simply waiting for a war, the whole lot of you': Moravia, *Two Women*, 321.

129 'the destruction of other people with the same feeling with which one enjoys the coming of spring and the flowers and the weather': Moravia, *Two Women*, 266.

129 *How can it be, she asks, that a ferocious Nazi, a man they encounter by chance in the mountains . . .*: Moravia, *Two Women*, 200-204.

130 'In short, it is almost better to have been born imperfect and gradually to become . . .': Moravia, *Two Women*, 299.

ACKNOWLEDGEMENTS

THE CHAPTERS IN THIS book nearly all arose in response to a request from a publication inviting me to think about the various crises—war, pandemic, soaring inequality—which have each cast such a dark shadow over the past years. I am grateful to all those who encouraged me to write in situations which have taken me to the limits of understanding. The first chapter on Albert Camus's *The Plague*, which gives this book its title, appeared in the *London Review of Books*, Volume 42, No. 9, 7 May 2020. The second chapter, on Freud and the death of his daughter, was delivered as the Annual Freud Memorial lecture, under the auspices of the Sigmund Freud Museum in Vienna, livestreamed—due to Covid-19—from the London Freud Museum on 23 September 2020. It was published in its first version in the *London Review of Books*, Volume 42, No. 22, 19 November 2020. Chapter Three, 'Living Death', was published in *Gagosian Quarterly*, Winter 2020, and Chapter Four,

'Life After Death', in *The Guardian*, 7 December 2021. Chapter Five, on Simone Weil, appeared in the *New York Review of Books*, Volume 69, No. 1, 13 January 2022. Each of them has been substantially revised and expanded for this book, taking into account as far as possible the rapidly evolving situation with which, since the first faint signs of the pandemic, the world has been faced.

I have continued to benefit from the input of Mary-Kay Wilmers and colleagues at the *London Review of Books*. I am grateful to editor and poet Jana Prikyl for welcoming me to the *New York Review of Books*. Thanks to Jamieson Webster for asking me to contribute to the *Gagosian*, and to Clare Longrigg for including me in the 200-year anniversary celebration of *The Guardian*. Special thanks to Monika Pessler and Daniela Finzi, Director and Research Director of the Sigmund Freud Museum in Vienna, first for inviting me to speak, and then for generously hosting the lecture in the face of considerable difficulties. Thanks are also due to Carol Siegel, Director of the London Freud Museum, for stepping in and creating a unique dialogue between London and Vienna. My thanks to Julia Kristeva, Pumla Gobodo-Madikizela, Judith Butler and Michael Parsons for their participation in the conversation that followed the lecture. Howard Caygill offered insight and much-needed support in relation to the extraordinary thinking of Simone Weil, who has turned into something of a guiding spirit through the book.

Once again, my thanks to Esther Leslie and other colleagues at the Birkbeck Institute for the Humanities whose perseverance in the ongoing, critical, project of the Humanities during these difficult times has felt exemplary. Likewise to Lisa Baraitser, Stephen Frosh and Daniel Pick for their unyielding commitment to the place of psychoanalysis in that project.

Thanks for the editorial skills of Milo Walls at Farrar, Straus and Giroux, who has once more been a pleasure to work with. I appreciate the kindness with which Mitzi Angel greeted the book. Tracy Bohan continues to offer support and friendship which has become more vital than ever. I am grateful to Jacques Testard for publishing the book at the extraordinary Fitzcarraldo Editions, where I join a list which inspires and daunts me in equal measure.

My much loved companions of life, thought and pleasure, who I have thanked before and in whose debt I will always be—including the one to whom this book is dedicated—each know who they are. Thank you all from the heart.

A Note About the Author

Jacqueline Rose is internationally recognized as one of the most important living feminist and cultural critics. She is a codirector of the Birkbeck Institute for the Humanities, a cofounder of Independent Jewish Voices, and a fellow of the British Academy and of the Royal Society of Literature. Rose is a frequent contributor to the *London Review of Books* and *The Guardian*, among many other publications. Her books include *Sexuality in the Field of Vision*, *The Haunting of Sylvia Plath*, *States of Fantasy*, *Women in Dark Times*, *Mothers: An Essay on Love and Cruelty*, and *On Violence and On Violence Against Women*.